DAVID

A MAN AFTER GOD'S OWN HEART

DAVİD

A MAN AFTER GOD'S OWN HEART

J. VERNON McGEE

THOMAS NELSON PUBLISHERS®

Nashville

MO OD RB VG

Library of Congress Cataloging-in-Publication Data

McGee, J. Vernon (John Vernon), 1904-1988
    David : a man after God's own heart / J. Vernon McGee
     p. cm.
    Includes bibliographical references.
    ISBN 0-7852-6821-9 (hc)
    1. David, King of Israel. 2. Bible. O.T.—Biography.
  I. Title
    BS580.D3 M36 2000
    222'.4092—dc21
    [B]

                                       99-087431

Printed in the United States of America
1 2 3 4 5 6 BVG 05 04 03 02 01 00

CONTENTS

INTRODUCTION

All too often, we view fantastic and supernatural stories from the Bible as just that—stories. If you attended Sunday school as a child, you probably have memories of sitting in a semicircle on the floor as your teacher introduced you to many fascinating people who lived long before Jesus was even born. More than likely, you had a favorite story—one that filled your young mind with wonder and made your eyes shine with anticipation at learning the outcome.

Few would argue with the assertion that one of the most popular Bible stories is that of David and the giant, Goliath. What little boy hasn't at some point imagined that he could use a slingshot as well as David? And who can deny being at one time or another the underdog facing a formidable giant of his own?

What we often fail to remember is that the stories and lives detailed in God's Word are there for the purpose of revealing deep, spiritual truths about God, His Son, and living the Christian life.

Set chronologically, the messages contained in this book focus on major episodes in the life of David, whose experiences not only tell the story of a life lived totally for God but also paint a picture of God's undying mercy, forgiveness, and love. Dr. McGee retells these stories in order to draw out applications on salvation, worship, obedience, faith, and God's discipline and forgiveness.

Have you ever wondered how David, guilty of adultery and murder, could be called a man after God's own heart? The overriding theme of this book is how a sinful and faulty man like David could accomplish great things for God because of his determined faith and intense love for the Shepherd of his soul.

As you read these pages, it is our hope that you will examine your own relationship with God and develop a heart for Him that echoes David's cry: "O God, You are my God; early will I seek You; my soul thirsts for You; my flesh longs for You" (Psalm 63:1).

*And Samuel said to Saul, "You have done fool-
ishly. You have not kept the commandment of
the LORD your God, which He commanded you.
For now the LORD would have established your
kingdom over Israel forever. But now your
kingdom shall not continue. The LORD has
sought for Himself a man after His own heart,
and the LORD has commanded him to be com-
mander over His people, because you have not
kept what the LORD commanded you."*

(1 Samuel 13:13–14)

*Now the LORD said to Samuel, "How long will
you mourn for Saul, seeing I have rejected him
from reigning over Israel? Fill your horn with
oil, and go; I am sending you to Jesse the
Bethlehemite. For I have provided Myself a
king among his sons." And Samuel said, "How
can I go? If Saul hears it, he will kill me." But
the LORD said, "Take a heifer with you, and say,
'I have come to sacrifice to the LORD.' Then
invite Jesse to the sacrifice, and I will show you
what you shall do; you shall anoint for Me the
one I name to you."*

*So Samuel did what the LORD said, and
went to Bethlehem. And the elders of the town
trembled at his coming, and said, "Do you come*

peaceably?" And he said, "Peaceably; I have
come to sacrifice to the LORD. Sanctify yourselves, and come with me to the sacrifice." Then
he consecrated Jesse and his sons, and invited
them to the sacrifice.

So it was, when they came, that he looked
at Eliab and said, "Surely the LORD'S anointed
is before Him!" But the LORD said to Samuel,
"Do not look at his appearance or at his physical stature, because I have refused him. For
the LORD does not see as man sees; for man
looks at the outward appearance, but the LORD
looks at the heart."

So Jesse called Abinadab, and made him
pass before Samuel. And he said, "Neither has
the LORD chosen this one." Then Jesse made
Shammah pass by. And he said, "Neither has
the LORD chosen this one." Thus Jesse made
seven of his sons pass before Samuel. And
Samuel said to Jesse, "The LORD has not chosen these."

And Samuel said to Jesse, "Are all the
young men here?" Then he said, "There
remains yet the youngest, and there he is, keeping the sheep." And Samuel said to Jesse,
"Send and bring him. For we will not sit down
till he comes here."

So he sent and brought him in. Now he was ruddy, with bright eyes, and good-looking. And the LORD said, "Arise, anoint him; for this is the one!" Then Samuel took the horn of oil and anointed him in the midst of his brothers; and the Spirit of the LORD came upon David from that day forward.

(1 Samuel 16:1–13)

CHAPTER 1

DAVID, THE GIANT KILLER

Perhaps the most familiar Bible story to every boy and girl who has attended Sunday school is that of David and Goliath. It is a thrilling action story. But the greater thrill is the splendid spiritual truths that are applicable to our present-day lives as believers. We often miss the spiritual overtones of this story because of the spectacular exploits of David. But the road to the spiritual is through the action recorded in Scripture, and I dare to retrace these events though they may be ever so familiar to you.

Let us begin by setting the stage on which the action took place. Israel was fighting their perennial and perpetual enemy, the Philistines. Even from the very beginning the Philistines were the enemy of Israel. After all, they were in that land first and had been put out, or at least moved to the edge, when the Israelites moved in. God warned Moses that He would not take Israel by the short route, the close route from Egypt up to Palestine, because of the presence of the Philistines. God knew that the Philistines were a fierce and warlike bunch, and He did not want His people to be discouraged by the sight of them. In reading Israel's history, we find that all during the time of the judges, and especially during the time of Samson, the Philistines were their enemy.

When we look at the story of David, we find that the Philistines were *still* the enemy of Israel. But at that time they had a giant of a man to champion their cause. His name, of course, was Goliath. It is interesting that the name *Goliath* means "soothsayer," which seems to indicate that he dealt with the occult, with that which was demonic. But we identify Goliath more with his size—he was a great hulk of a man with unmatched physical strength. We are told that he measured six cubits, so if we are accurate about the length of a cubit, Goliath must have been somewhere around nine feet and one span, a span being about nine inches. So he was not Mr.

Five Feet–Five Inches but Mr. Nine Feet–Nine Inches. He was a big boy—almost ten feet tall—and could have played center or forward on any basketball team!

As the story opens, the war had come to a stalemate because of the presence of this giant. The armed forces of Israel were on one side of a hill, the Philistine troops on the side of another hill, and down in between there was a valley. The men of Israel were astonished and intimidated because each day Goliath paraded up and down the valley, challenging the Israelites to send out a man to fight him:

Then he stood and cried out to the armies of Israel, and said to them, "Why have you come out to line up for battle? Am I not a Philistine, and you the servants of Saul? Choose a man for yourselves, and let him come down to me. If he is able to fight with me and kill me, then we will be your servants. But if I prevail against him and kill him, then you shall be our servants and serve us . . . I defy the armies of Israel this day; give me a man, that we may fight together." When Saul and all Israel heard these words of the Philistine, they were

dismayed and greatly afraid. (1 Samuel
17:8–11)

The men of Israel cringed in cowardly fashion at
the boasting and braggadocio of this man. So after
forty days of taunting, no one had accepted
Goliath's challenge.

It was at this juncture that Jesse, a father
with three sons in the battle, sent his youngest
son, David, to the scene of battle to take provi-
sions for his brothers and also a token to the captain of the host of Israel. While David was in the
camp, Goliath came forth, and David heard his
speech. Believe me, David was incensed! He
spoke to the man that stood by him, asking,

**What shall be done for the man who kills
this Philistine and takes away the
reproach from Israel? For who is this
uncircumcised Philistine, that he should
defy the armies of the living God?** (v. 26)

That's brave talk for a shepherd boy! But David
was one who had a consuming passion for God.
Oh, David had his faults and David committed
sin, but I believe that no man ever had the feeling and the love and the consuming passion for

God that this man had. Amazing person, David was! And Goliath's challenge didn't send David down behind a rock to hide in fear. He wanted something done about it.

Obviously David's talk was not pleasing to his oldest brother (you can imagine an older brother in a situation like this):

> *Now Eliab his oldest brother heard when he spoke to the men; and Eliab's anger was aroused against David, and he said, "Why did you come down here? And with whom have you left those few sheep in the wilderness? I know your pride and the insolence of your heart, for you have come down to see the battle."* (v. 28)

It's quite interesting to notice that Eliab could get angry at David, but he didn't get angry at the Philistine. But David *was* angry at the Philistine, and he wanted something done about it. King Saul got word that David was interested in offering up his services, so David was brought before him.

> *Then David said to Saul, "Let no man's heart fail because of him; your servant will go and fight with this Philistine."* (v. 32)

Since Saul now had a volunteer, he was willing to take on the giant!

Of course, the natural thing to do first was to dress David out in the king's armor. David was just a boy, however, so the armor didn't fit and the sword was too heavy. But that wasn't really the problem. The problem was that David could not use the instruments and methods of this world to fight the giant. So David said, "I can't fight with these because I haven't tested them. I will just have to fight with the equipment I'm used to."

What a lesson there is for us in this! Let's not try to be something we are not or try to do something we are really not called to do. If God has called you to use a slingshot, friend, don't try to use a sword. If God has called you to speak, then speak. If God has called you to do something else, well, do that. If God has called you to sing, then sing. But if He has not called you to sing, for goodness sake, don't do it. Too many people are trying to use a sword when the slingshot is really more their size.

Now I think we ought to make something very clear. I've heard it argued that it really was an accident when David's rock smashed Goliath in just the right place. May I say to you that David knew exactly where he was going to put that stone! He was an expert at using a slingshot. There was no question about it in his mind, and he had no qualms whatsoever.

David was not the only man in Israel who knew how to use a sling; it was a common skill in those days. Let's go back to the twentieth chapter of the Book of Judges. There we are told this:

Among all this people were seven hundred select men who were left-handed; every one could sling a stone at a hair's breadth and not miss. (Judges 20:16)

This means that there were seven hundred men who could each be given a stone and could put down seven hundred hairs, I don't know at how many paces—it would have to be pretty close for me! But regardless of how far away it was, those seven hundred men could break those hairs. So if you feel that David's feat was more or less accidental, you are wrong because David was an expert. Just think of the days and years he had spent out beyond the woods with his father's sheep, using his slingshot to keep them from straying. David himself said that when a lion or a bear came to take a lamb out of the flock, he would strike and kill it and deliver the lamb out of the mouth! And what if he should miss? Well, he became so skilled that he didn't miss!

I think the thing we should understand is this: David had absolute confidence that God would deliver him.

> *Moreover David said, "The LORD, who delivered me from the paw of the lion and from the paw of the bear, He will deliver me from the hand of this Philistine." And Saul said to David, "Go, and the LORD be with you!"* (1 Samuel 17:37)

David knew that he could not use the weapons of this world to fight the battle. He had to use his own weapons, his own methods—those in which God had schooled him. The believer today needs to recognize that the world can be overcome only by faith and confidence in God.

Let's move ahead to the fortieth verse, as David went forth:

> *Then he took his staff in his hand; and he chose for himself five smooth stones from the brook, and put them in a shepherd's bag, in a pouch which he had, and his*

sling was in his hand. And he drew near to the Philistine.

We are told here that he took with him five smooth stones. Some people believe that David chose five stones so that if he missed his first shot, he could use one or all of the others. But David did not intend to miss, friend. Then why did he select five stones? The answer is found in 2 Samuel 21:22: "These four were born to the giant in Gath, and fell by the hand of David and by the hand of his servants." When the giant Goliath paraded up and down each day, he had four sons as big as he was over yonder in the Philistine camp. And they watched their papa go up and down every day. So David took five stones, one for each boy. But the boys didn't come out that day, although they did later, and David and his men got rid of them then. But David had only one stone for Goliath. What a tremendous thing!

Now when the giant saw that David was just a boy, he became boastful and insulting.

And when the Philistine looked about and saw David, he disdained him; for he was only a youth, ruddy and good-looking. So the Philistine said to David, "Am I a dog, that you come to me with sticks?" And the Philistine cursed David by his gods. And the Philistine said to David, "Come to me, and I will give your flesh to the birds of the air and the beasts of the field!" (1 Samuel 17:42–44)

In other words, "Go on back. I don't want *you!* I'm not moving to the cradle yet! I don't want to fight you—you are only a boy." Then Goliath used the names of his pagan gods to curse David. Notice how David, just a young man, answered him:

You come to me with a sword, with a spear, and with a javelin. But I come to you in the name of the Lord of hosts, the God of the armies of Israel, whom you have defied. This day the Lord will deliver you into my hand, and I will strike you and take your head from you. And this day I will give the carcasses of the camp of the Philistines to the birds of the air and the wild beasts of the earth, that all the earth may know that there is a God in Israel.

> *Then all this assembly shall know that the
> LORD does not save with sword and spear;
> for the battle is the LORD'S, and He will
> give you into our hands.* (vv. 45–47)

David's faith and confidence were absolutely in
God. I don't need to finish the story—I'm sure you
know how it ends. God gave David the victory.
The battle was the Lord's, and the giant was
delivered into David's hands.

May I say that I am now eager to draw spiri-
tual lessons from this event. In the Scriptures,
David is a picture of Christ, he is a small adum-
bration of Christ. If you follow the words of our
Lord very carefully, you will notice, when Jesus
was rebuked by His critics, how often He said,
"Have you ever read what David did under similar
circumstances?" He was constantly referring to
David. Remember, also, that He was in David's
ancestral line and was considered the son of
David. Someday He shall occupy the throne of
David. So David is just a small picture of Christ.
Likewise, David also represents the believer in the
Lord Jesus Christ. Further—and here is a place
where some might disagree with me—I believe the
giant represents the world, and I think King Saul
represents Satan.

The final conflict will eventually be between God and Satan—David and Saul. But for now it's between believers and the world—David and Goliath. When you and I first come to Christ, the world is our enemy. I'm not talking about the world of *people*. It is the world *system*, the cosmos—which includes governments, educational systems, and entertainments—that is the enemy of the believer today. Our Lord made it very clear. Notice what He said in John 15:18–19:

> *If the world hates you, you know that it hated Me before it hated you. If you were of the world, the world would love its own. Yet because you are not of the world, but I chose you out of the world, therefore the world hates you.*

Something is wrong with your testimony if the world loves you. Something is wrong today with your life if you are living arm in arm with the world. John again said in 1 John 2:15–16:

> *Do not love the world or the things in the world. If anyone loves the world, the love of the Father is not in him. For all that is in the world—the lust of the flesh, the lust*

of the eyes, and the pride of life—is not of the Father but is of the world.

We are to be *in* the world but not *of* it.

David treated Goliath as an enemy—an enemy of himself, an enemy of his people, and an enemy of God. What a difference between David and Samson! Samson treated the Philistines as friends—he even married one of them. This distinguishes literally thousands of believers today—some are Samsons and some are Davids. David said, "The Philistine is my enemy, and I must have a victory over him." Samson said, in effect, "The way to do it is to start a United Nations, and we'll all get together and get along just fine." My beloved, that thinking was the downfall and destruction of Samson. But David had the victory.

Our Lord says you are *in* the world but you are not *of* the world. You and I cannot fight the world with its own weapons and methods. David found that out. Notice again what he said to Goliath:

You come to me with a sword, with a spear, and with a javelin. But I come to you in the name of the LORD of hosts, the God of

*the armies of Israel, whom you have
defied.* (1 Samuel 17:45)

David's words are tremendously important: "You
are coming to me with the weapons of the world,
but I am not fighting you with the weapons of the
world." We do not fight the world today with the
type of weapons it uses. We must have a spiritual
weapon, and that weapon is faith in God:

*This day the LORD will deliver you into my
hand, and I will strike you and take your
head from you. And this day I will give the
carcasses of the camp of the Philistines to
the birds of the air and the wild beasts of
the earth, that all the earth may know that
there is a God in Israel.* (v. 46)

May I say to you, that was the faith of David!
Remember what the apostle John said:

*For whatever is born of God overcomes the
world. And this is the victory that has
overcome the world—our faith.* (1 John 5:4)

You and I cannot use the weapons of the world.
But by *faith* today we can overcome.

Now I come to a verse where we want to pause:

Then all this assembly shall know that the LORD does not save with sword and spear; for the battle is the LORD's, and He will give you into our hands. (1 Samuel 17:47)

The battle is the Lord's. Joshua learned the same lesson when, instead of fighting a battle, he marched around the city of Jericho for seven days. By *faith* the walls of Jericho fell down! Why? Because the battle is the Lord's. David said to King Saul, "I can't use this armor; I don't want this sword. I go forward in the name of the Lord." And though he was an expert with that sling, his confidence was in God. Friend, if we are ever to have a victory over the world, we will have to learn that the battle is the Lord's. *He* has to get the victory over the world. You and I cannot.

CHAPTER 2

WATER FROM THE WELL OF BETHLEHEM

There are many unsung heroes of the Bible, and among them are the mighty men of David. Among the many who were chief, we are going to look at three. These three mighty men are not only unsung, they are unidentified. They are introduced to us in the Second Book of Samuel:

> *Then three of the thirty chief men went down at harvest time and came to David at the cave of Adullam. And the troop of Philistines encamped in the Valley of Rephaim.* (2 Samuel 23:13)

Their names are not given. Alexandre Dumas gives the names of the Three Musketeers, but we do not have the names of these three mighty men of David who did a tremendous and courageous thing for David at that time.

Did you know that there are in the church today a great company of unsung, unnamed, and unknown heroes?

I remember that when I was still a student in seminary (in fact, I was graduating that spring) the Westminster Presbyterian Church in Atlanta, Georgia, was without a pastor. They'd had a great deal of difficulty in the church. It was torn by internal strife. They had called Peter Marshall, a great man of God who would later become the chaplain of the United States Senate. They wanted to get somebody to be the interim pastor who could not hurt the church, and they figured that a seminary student would be the one. So when they asked the seminary to recommend someone, I was sent to preach until Peter Marshall came as the pastor of that church.

I will never forget that first Sunday. It was probably the most difficult message I've ever given. The congregation was sitting there on the very edge of their pews waiting for something to be said that would cause more strife and difficulty. The steeple on that church was ready to blow off at any moment. I never will forget how discouraged I was after the morning message and again after the evening message.

All week I toyed with the idea of telling them I wouldn't be back anymore. But I continued on, and the next Sunday morning it was the same thing. However, that second Sunday night God moved in, and we saw a real working of the Holy Spirit.

After the message, a dear lady (a little tiny lady, she was) came up to me and in a trembling voice said, "Young man, I saw the problem you had last Sunday morning. I have been getting up early for more than twenty years to pray for this church and its service, but after I saw that you were really in difficulty, I got up this Sunday morning an hour earlier and I prayed for you and for the service. Tonight I'm certainly rejoicing in what has happened."

I have thought of that little lady many times since then. I don't even remember her name. Many of us have heard of Peter Marshall, but I wonder if someday she might be the one who will get the credit for the ministry he had at that church. I know she will certainly get the credit for the ministry I had there, because into that coldness this little lady came with her prayers.

She's one of those unsung, unnamed heroines of the faith.

We have multitudes sitting in congregations throughout the land (some cannot even attend services because of an infirmity of the flesh) who are the important ones. Their names have not appeared on the front page of the bulletin; they're not listed with the staff; perhaps they are never mentioned even on an inside page of the bulletin. Some of them never come out in public at all, but they really are the ones who are undergirding the work of God with prayer and with their support. May I say, there's a great company of unnamed and unsung heroes of the faith.

That will be one of the glories of the day when we stand in Christ's presence and He brings His reward with Him. We're going to see countless numbers of people about whom we have never read in the Bible; we never read about them at all in church history; we didn't know they were in our church. But they were the ones who were the heroes and heroines. They were the ones who were standing back, fighting the battle of faith.

David, we find, had three such men. They are not identified, but they are three of the mightiest men that you'll find on the pages of Scripture. In this message I want to answer two very simple questions relative to these mighty men. The first one is, *Who were they?* and the second is, *What did they do?* I want you, as best you can, to get acquainted with these mighty men of David, for they're worth knowing. When I get to heaven, I want to meet every one of them. I want to sit down and talk with each one about the exploits that he did for God while under David's command.

Who Were They?

There are thirty-seven mighty men listed in 2 Samuel 23. If you'll turn to the corresponding passage in 1 Chronicles 11, you'll find there are actually forty-eight listed, eleven more than are listed in 2 Samuel. Neither this list nor the one in Chronicles is a complete listing. It is as though God tore just one page out of His roster in heaven and put it down here in His Word to let you and me know that there were men and women back in those days who lived for Him and who carried out exploits for God.

I want you to notice these men who are called in the Hebrew *gibbor*, which means "powerful." They were powerful in the sense that they were in the will of God and they were doing God's will.

Over in 1 Chronicles 11:10 they are called "heads of the mighty men," which would indicate that these are in the upper echelon; these were the brass, if you please. They performed feats for God. On these imposing rosters of mighty men are three, identified individually as "one of the three mighty men." These three stand at the head of the entire list.

Now I want you to notice where these men came from. If we are going to know who they are, we will have to know how in the world they got lined up with David. Back when David was first starting out—after he was anointed and after he was driven out by Saul—we read:

> *And everyone who was in distress, everyone who was in debt, and everyone who was discontented gathered to him. So he became captain over them. And there were about four hundred men with him.* (1 Samuel 22:2)

These are the men who came to David during the days of his rejection, in that interval from the time the anointing oil was put on him until he assumed the throne.

In that period when Saul hunted him, David was disciplined and trained of God out yonder in the dens and caves of the earth. You can find in many of the psalms expressions that depict David's experiences during that period in his life. For instance, he said in one of his psalms that he was hunted like a partridge. In other words, David said, "It was open season on me. Saul was out looking for me, and I was like a little bird being hunted." Then you find him saying this:

> *I am like a pelican of the wilderness; I am like an owl of the desert.* (Psalm 102:6)

Did you ever take a look at a pelican? I always think of this verse when I see a pelican. The pelican apparently has never read *How to Win Friends and Influence People*, for he is the most sad, doleful-looking creature—looks like he just lost his mother. That's the way David said he was during that period. Further, David said, "I was like the owl of the desert"—that is, at night he had to stand guard, he had to watch. He made this statement also:

> *My soul is among lions; I lie among the sons of men who are set on fire, whose teeth are spears and arrows, and their tongue a sharp sword . . . They have prepared a net for my steps.* (Psalm 57:4, 6)

My, I tell you, that is a picture, is it not? And he's not speaking of the lions out in the wilderness but of the enemies that were round about him. It was during this period of being hunted and hounded, the period of his rejection, that he gathered these men about him.

He made the cave of Adullam his headquarters. Adullam was between Hebron and Philistia. It was in the canyon that was called Rephaim, which means the Valley of Giants. In this particular place David set up his headquarters, and men began to drift in and come to him. Three types of men came: those who were in distress, those who were in debt, and those who were discontented.

We find that there were four hundred men at the very beginning, then we're told: "So David and his men, about six hundred . . ." (1 Samuel 23:13). You see, in just a brief period of time two hundred more men had joined him. I have no notion how many men were following David, but it was a small army by the time he came to the throne.

Those Who Were in Distress

The men who came to him were, first of all, those who were in distress. Saul was in power, and David was rejected and out yonder in the caves. Saul persecuted and oppressed many of his subjects and these men who were in distress wanted deliverance and relief. They heard of David and went out to him. Many a man came into the camp of David in desperation and said, "I have been hounded like you have been hounded. I have been hated as you have been hated, and I have come to join up with you."

What a picture, my beloved. What a picture that is today of the Lord Jesus Christ, for these are the days of *His* rejection. He is hunted and hounded on this earth. The Lord Jesus Christ said:

If the world hates you, you know that it hated Me before it hated you. (John 15:18)

You and I are living in a day when Christ is hated in the world. If you are really on His side, you never will be voted the most popular person in your community. (I do not mean by this that you are to become objectionable or unlovely, because I think you become the opposite if you belong to Him.) But if you are His, the world will not love you because He is not loved by this world. We are living in the days of His rejection.

Men and women today who are in distress, who feel the burden of their sin upon them and need a deliverance, come to Him today and enlist under His banner. Multitudes have done so. John Bunyan said that when he came to Christ he did not come just as a sinner, but there was borne in upon him the conviction that he was a sinner from the crown of his head to the soles of his feet, that he was sick with sin, that he was like a putrid, running sore in God's sight. And in his desperation he went to Christ. All of us who are in distress, who see that we are undone, who realize there is no help or hope within us or among men, need to step out in faith and come to the only Deliverer, the only Savior, and be identified under the banner of Jesus Christ, for we are living in the days of His rejection.

Someone years ago said of David, "He's a remarkable type of the Divine Prince." You see, David had several opportunities to destroy Saul, but he did not take them. He said that Saul was God's anointed and that God, not he, would have to deal with him.

While Christ is rejected today, Satan is the prince of this world. I wish Christians really believed this. Satan today is the prince of this world. He is the one prowling about like "a roaring lion, seeking whom he may devour" (1 Peter 5:8). He had the audacity to say to Jesus Christ: "I will give You all the kingdoms of this world if

You will fall down and worship me" (see Matthew 4:8–9). And, my friend, if he didn't have the kingdoms, our Lord would have called his hand. But Satan does have them; he is a usurper here today. And may I add this: God could put him out in a moment's time, but Satan is permitted to continue by the permissive will of God. Satan is the one who causes our problems and our difficulties in the world. You will have to leave his bailiwick, you will have to get out from under his rulership, and you will have to turn to Christ if you want to get rid of the distress of your sin today. We are told that over fifteen million tranquilizers are being sold yearly. They may help you, my friend, but they won't get rid of your distresses. Only Jesus Christ can give us peace and relief from our distress in this day.

Those Who Were in Debt

There was another group that came to David—those who were in debt. You see, God attempted to protect His people from debt because in that day a man in debt was actually in a terrible predicament. This is the law that God gave:

If you lend money to any of My people who are poor among you, you shall not be like a moneylender to him; you shall not charge him interest. (Exodus 22:25)

God protected the poor. But apparently Saul did not enforce the Mosaic Law. And you'll find out that even later on, during the time of Elisha, this was said:

A certain woman of the wives of the sons of the prophets cried out to Elisha, saying, "Your servant my husband is dead, and you know that your servant feared the Lord. And the creditor is coming to take my two sons to be his slaves." (2 Kings 4:1)

In Saul's day, many men in debt were in danger of being sold into slavery. But before they could be taken into slavery, they ran off and joined up with David.

May I say that you and I are in debt. Every person is in debt. Right now the national debt is such that every person in America owes several thousands of dollars. That is, it would take that to get America out of debt today. So why don't you pay your share? Well, most of us can't pay; we are in debt. However, I'm not talking about that kind of debt. I'm talking about a debt that sin has put us under. Our Lord taught His disciples to pray, "Forgive us our debts," because we are in debt. And it was Paul who said to the Galatians,

And I testify again to every man who becomes circumcised that he is a debtor to keep the whole law. (Galatians 5:3)

You and I today are debtors to measure up to God's standard, and it is a debt we cannot pay. Paul says that we can't; according to the flesh, we would never measure up.

Therefore, brethren, we are debtors—not to the flesh, to live according to the flesh. (Romans 8:12)

If you attempt to live by the flesh, you will find yourself so far in debt you will never be able to ransom yourself out. But the hymn has it right: "*He* paid the debt and set us free."[1] When you and I were hopelessly and helplessly in debt, the Lord Jesus Christ went to the cross and paid that debt, and that is what forgiveness is today.

Not far from New York, in a cemetery lone,
Close guarding its grave, stands a simple
  headstone,
And all the inscription is one word alone—

  Forgiven.

No sculptor's fine art hath embellish'd its
  form,
But constantly there, through the calm
  and the storm,
It beareth this word from a poor fallen worm—

  Forgiven.

It shows not the date of the silent one's birth,
Reveals not his frailties, nor lies of his worth,
But speaks out the tale from his few feet
  of earth—

  Forgiven.

The death is unmention'd, the name is untold,
Beneath lies the body, corrupted and cold,
Above rests his spirit, at home in the fold—

  Forgiven.

And when from the heavens the Lord shall
  descend,

This stranger shall rise and in glory ascend,
Well-known and befriended, to sing without
end—

Forgiven.
—Author unknown

As far as we know, David never paid the debt of any of his mighty men, but the Lord Jesus Christ went to the cross and paid your debt. Can you say today, "I'm forgiven"? Can you say, "I am a forgiven sinner; He has forgiven me"? That's the only way in the world you will ever get the debt canceled.

Those Who Were Discontented

Then the third group—those who were discontented—came to David. They were bitter of soul, discontented with life. All over the world today there is a restlessness. It has been growing in a mighty crescendo since World War II. We've seen it break out in the Near East, then the Far East, then in South America and Africa; we've seen it break out in North America, in Europe, and on every continent. There is a restlessness in the hearts of men and women. Because of the corruption and injustice of the world, a great many people are seeking a change. Are you discontented today?

Many in Israel who were attempting to make an honest living saw the injustice of Saul's reign, saw the way things were going, and one day dropped their tools, left it all, and went out to join up with David. And many today who are discontented with this world know that they can't find anything that satisfies in any of the ideologies of this world. A man who is an ex-communist said to me one day, "McGee, I've tasted them all, and they won't satisfy. It wasn't until I came to Christ that I found what I wanted."

My friend, today Jesus Christ is sending out the invitation. He is gathering a group of mighty men around Him during these days of His rejection. Personally, I think the greatest period in the life of David was the time when he was gathering mighty men around him. Oh, if we could only sense it! So many of us who are fundamental say, "If only the Lord would come"—and believe me, I wish He would. But when we get up there and look back down here, we are going to find these were the greatest days to live. I'm afraid many of us will have regrets and say, "If I could only go back and live my life over again, I'd live for God."

There was a young man who came to speak to me, and I could see the look of discontentment in his eyes. He said, "I don't want to do this in life, and I don't want to do that in life. I want to give my life to God." Discontented with what the world calls success, he wanted to live for God. Oh, if we had more like that! Those are the ones who will come to Christ. Men like that came to David. Those were his mighty men.

What Did They Do?

Now what did these mighty men do? Well, they were men of unquestioned loyalty to David, men of undying courage, men of unfeigned love. Every one of them loved David personally. Every one was a man of indefatigable zeal. Oh, how each would go all-out for David! Every one of these men carried out exploits for God.

Here is the story of the three mightiest men. They came to David when he was in the cave of Adullam, while he was rejected. Actually, David was in a bad spot at this particular time because not only was Saul hunting for him, but the Philistines had made a flank movement, had bypassed him, and had come into Bethlehem. They had taken Bethlehem at harvest season.

It was hot and dusty, and David, as he stood there that day in the cave of Adullam, was thirsty! But this is all he said:

Oh, that someone would give me a drink of the water from the well of Bethlehem, which is by the gate! (2 Samuel 23:15)

You see, Bethlehem was his hometown, and in his thirst he thought of the water at home. He simply said, "Oh, if I just had a drink out of that well."

Unfortunately, most of our young people today know nothing about wells. They get their "purified" water out of a spigot, and it all tastes the same—bad. But some of us were raised in the country. One year I went back to the little town in which I had lived as a boy—I'm sorry I took my wife because she has never ceased kidding me about that place. It's not very big—not more than a hundred people live there today. And I went up to the place my dad had built and to the well that he had dug. The old windmill was still there, and it still made the same noise as it was pumping up the water. I asked the people living there if I could go out and get a drink. They didn't mind, so I went and put my mouth under the spigot that was coming right up out of the well. It's "gyp" water, west Texas "gyp" water. Did you ever drink "gyp" water? I was raised on it, and honestly I never tasted a chocolate malted milk that was as good as that. Oh, that water was delicious! It took me back to my boyhood, and right now I'm thirsty just thinking about it. I wish I had a big jug of that water right now, water from the well in Ira, Texas. That's good water if you were raised on it—if you weren't raised on it, you couldn't stand the stuff.

David said, "Oh, if I only had a drink of water from the well at Bethlehem!" Now will you notice that David did not give a command. He could have, but he did not call a soldier before him and say, "Listen. Your order for the day is to get through the enemy lines and get me water from the well at Bethlehem." David would never do that. Just as a wish of his heart, he said, "Oh, if I could only get water from the well." But David's soldiers so loved him and were so loyal to him that they treated his wishes as if they were commands. These three mighty men heard him. I suppose one said to the other, "Did you hear what he said? He wants a drink from the well at Bethlehem." And the other one said, "Well, you know, the Philistines are as thick as hawks over there." And the third one said, "Yes, but David wants the water." So all three started out. And, my friend, they got the water.

> *So the three mighty men broke through the camp of the Philistines, drew water from the well of Bethlehem that was by the gate, and took it and brought it to David.*
> (2 Samuel 23:16)

They went after it, and they brought it back to David—it was almost a superhuman feat that they performed.

May I remind you that the Lord Jesus, when He was down here upon this earth, expressed a wish. He said to the woman at the well, "Give Me a drink" (John 4:7). The record does not say that she ever gave Him a drink. (A little later, in verse 32, He said to His disciples, "I have food to eat of which you do not know," and I'm sure that she hadn't given Him anything to eat, either.) He didn't get a drink when He asked for it. On the cross He said, "I thirst," and they gave Him vinegar to drink. My friend, we think that was bad, but *we* treat the commands of Christ today as if they were just His wishes and whims. "Lord, You say to take the gospel to the ends of the earth. Well, if we get around to it, we'll try. And I hope You'll appreciate what we're doing right now." David's men treated his wishes as if they were commands; we treat the commands of Christ as if they were only wishes.

These three mighty men risked their lives, broke through the lines of the Philistines, got that water and brought it back to David. Now notice David's strange reaction:

> *Nevertheless he would not drink it, but poured it out to the LORD. And he said, "Far be it from me, O LORD, that I should do this! Is this not the blood of the men who went in jeopardy of their lives?" Therefore he would not drink it. These things were done by the three mighty men.*
> (2 Samuel 23:16, 17)

These three men brought back the water, and they said to David, "Here it is." I think every one of them was bloody. They had had to fight to get through the lines, get that water, and get back. And David saw what they had done. My, how he was moved! "Why, men," he said, "I couldn't stand here and drink this water—it would be just like drinking your blood. That water represents your life, the life that you were willing to lay down for me." But David recognized the bravery of these men. He said, "I can't drink it. I offer it as a libation unto God. I pour it out as a drink offering to God."

Oh, what a lesson is here! In Psalm 22 we discover that on the cross the Lord Jesus Christ said certain things you'll not find in the Gospels, and one of the things He said was, "I am poured out like water" (verse 14). He was a drink-offering. He is the Mighty Man of God—He is called "The Mighty God" by Isaiah. He came over the battlements of heaven into Satan's territory. On the cross He poured out His life like water in order that there might be water from heaven for the souls of men and women who are thirsty. And today He says,

If anyone thirsts, let him come to Me and drink. (John 7:37)

Ho! Everyone who thirsts, come to the waters. (Isaiah 55:1)

The invitation is to everyone, but it's limited to those who are thirsty. Are you thirsty today? Are you discontented? Do you feel in debt to God? Oh, friend, go to Him! He has the water of life.

It was toward the end of the Civil War when the forces of Generals Grant and Lee were locked in deadly, mortal combat at Richmond. All during the day both sides had gone back and forth over the battlefield. And in late afternoon out on the battlefield lay boys in blue and boys in gray, dying. A young Confederate lieutenant went to his captain and said, "You hear those men out there. They're wounded and crying for water. I'm going to take it to them." The captain said, "It'll mean your death. It's a foolish thing to do." He replied, "I don't care. I'm going to take them water." So he went around to the other men and they emptied their canteens into his, then he crawled out over the battlements, out into that no-man's land, and crawled from one soldier to another, giving them water.

Out over the battlements of heaven came the Son of God. And He brought, not a canteen of water, but His own life's blood that He shed while on the cross. Today those who are thirsty can drink—but you have to be thirsty.

David's mighty men were inspired to do these heroic deeds because of what David had done— slaying the giant and other acts of bravery. Paul said something that we don't get in the King James translation of Philippians 2:17. The Amplified New Testament reads:

> *Even if [my lifeblood] must be poured out as a libation on the sacrificial offering of your faith [to God], still I am glad [to do it] and congratulate you all on [your share in] it.* (AMPLIFIED)

Paul said, "I want my life to be like a drink offering, taken and poured on the offering of Christ." In the Old Testament, that is the way the drink offering was used. It was poured on the burnt offering, and it just went up in steam, of course. Paul said, "I want my life to be spent just like that for Christ—nothing for myself, but my life to be put on the sacrifice of Christ." That's the kind of individual God needs today, and the kind God wants. Paul wanted his life to be like that, and I believe it was.

Dwight L. Moody, as a young man, heard an obscure preacher by the name of Henry Varley make this statement: "The world has yet to see what God can do with a man who is fully yielded to Him."[2] By the way he lived his life, I imagine Moody said to himself, "By the grace of God, I'll be that man." But by the end of his earthly career, I am convinced that even Dwight L. Moody had to say, "The world has yet to see what God can do with a man who is fully yielded to him."

My friend, today this low level on which Christians are living is not pleasing to God. Today He is calling you to a higher plane. But if you come to Christ, you will first have to come to Him in your distress, a lost sinner. You'll have to come recognizing you owe God a debt and are discontented with this world. If you are enjoying drinking at the cistern of this world, you will never come to Him; but if you are thirsty, come to Him, the One who can and will satisfy.

And then the next thing is to do what David's mighty men did. Those mighty men loved David—oh, how they loved him. To them his wish was a command. David was a wonderful man. Our problem today is that a great many people get their theology right—oh, they're so fundamental—but they are not in love with Christ. That great big fisherman, Simon Peter, said, "Whom having not seen you love" (1 Peter 1:8). And our Lord's question to Simon Peter in John 21:16 is His question to you and me today: "Do you love Me?" Earlier Jesus had made this

statement: "If you love Me, keep My commandments" (John 14:15). Our obedience is proof of
our love for Him.

Oh, to be in love with Jesus Christ today!

CHAPTER 3

DOING THE RIGHT THING THE WRONG WAY

There are so many outstanding episodes in the life of David that it would be difficult to pick out the greatest one. But if I were permitted to put down that day which is the greatest day in the life of David, I would choose the day he brought the ark of the covenant up to Jerusalem—that is, when he brought it up the *right* way. That, for David, was the high day in his life.

You see, the ark of the covenant was tremendously important. It denoted the very presence of God with the people of Israel. The ark of the covenant is the best word-picture of Christ we have in the Old Testament.

It was only a chest: a box that was two and a half cubits long, one and a half cubits wide, and a cubit and a half high. It was made of acacia wood, but the wood didn't show because it was covered completely, inside and out, by gold. So the ark was both a gold box and a wooden box. Likewise, Christ was both God and Man in one blessed Person. That box speaks of the Person of Christ, His "hypostatic union," for He was both God and Man in one.

In that box were three very important items. There were, first of all, the stone tablets of the covenant, which speak of the life of Christ. He is the only Person who ever lived on this earth who kept the Ten Commandments. He is the only one who ever fulfilled the Law in all its detail, for He said He had come to fulfill the Law. Then there was the golden pot of manna. According to John 6:32–33, that pot of manna speaks of His death, for He said,

> *Most assuredly, I say to you, Moses did not give you the bread from heaven, but My Father gives you the true bread from heaven. For the bread of God is He who comes down from heaven and gives life to the world.* (John 6:32–33)

And finally there was Aaron's rod that budded which, in my view, speaks of the resurrection of Christ, for that rod was as lifeless as the rest, but it came to life with buds, blossoms, and almonds. So we have in the ark the glorious, blessed Person of Christ, and we have His work of redemption.

But that's not all. To crown it all was the top of the box, called "the mercy seat." It was the most highly ornamented part of the tabernacle. Bezalel, who was an artificer in gold, was given a special enduement of power of the Holy Spirit just to craft this impressive item. It was a beautiful thing! The wings of two cherubim stretched across the top, and those two cherubim of gold looked down on the mercy seat on which was blood. The presence of blood is what made it a mercy seat. That blood spoke of the fact that Christ would shed His blood so that God, a holy God, might be merciful to you and to me.

So, as you can see, we have in the ark one of the most glorious pictures of Christ.

Now, the overweening desire of David's life was that he might build God a temple in Jerusalem in which to house the ark of the covenant. When he took the city of Jerusalem from the Jebusites he said, "In this place I'll make my capital, I'll establish my home. And this is the place where I want

God's temple to be built" (see 1 Chronicles 11:4–5 and 2 Samuel 7:1–2). It is interesting to note that David's choice of Jerusalem was God's choice long before. God had told Moses when they were still out in the wilderness,

> *Three times a year all your males shall appear before the LORD your God in the place which He chooses.* (Deuteronomy 16:16)

That place was Jerusalem. You see, David was a man after God's own heart, so David's choice was God's choice, and God's choice was David's choice.

Once the city belonged to him, David's great ambition was to bring up the ark. Years before, the Philistines had captured it, but they endured such trouble and destruction that after seven months they returned the ark to Israel, to a little place eight miles to the west of Jerusalem called Kirjath Jearim. The ark had been taken to the house of Abinadab, and for twenty years there it stayed (see 1 Samuel 5:1–7:2). David had it in his heart to go get the ark and bring it to Jerusalem.

Maybe that doesn't impress you. But, may I say to you, David had a passion and a love for God that has seldom been equaled and never has been surpassed! David loved God as probably no other ever has. He had a desire for God, and he had a capacity for God.

Today we go through a lot of form and ceremony, even in our Bible-teaching churches. In most churches we start in a perfunctory sort of way, maybe by standing and singing the "Doxology." How many of us at that moment are actually worshiping Him? You see, friends, all we have in our churches is the sum total of each individual's spiritual warmth. One of the reasons our churches seem cold is that when you bring together several hundred backslidden church members, another several hundred indifferent church members, and another several hundred that have no notion of what it is to *worship* God, the spiritual temperature goes down to freezing.

By way of illustration, a little girl had gone to church with her family, and her mother wanted to make sure she had been paying attention, so she asked her, "Dear, what was the text this morning?" The little girl thought for a moment or two, then she said, "Many were cold, but a few were frozen." May I say to you, that was not exactly a quotation from Scripture, but it probably was very accurate. Many of us today, instead of called and chosen, are spiritually cold and a few are frozen. For this reason it's very difficult for you and me to enter into the heart and the thinking of King David.

Let me pass on to you some of the things that were in his heart, which he revealed in song. To do so we have to go to the Book of Psalms to find out what he really thought and what went on in his heart. Listen to him:

> *I will praise You with my whole heart.*
> (Psalm 138:1)

If you think this man David served God half-heartedly, you are wrong. David gave Him everything he had. In most churches today we don't dare exhibit our feelings. A man in my congregation came to me once and asked, "Is it all right for me to say 'Amen' in this church?" I said, "Yes." "Well," he said, "I did that the other day, and I got several very antagonistic looks." So I advised him to just shut his eyes when he said it.

Oh, my friend, if you and I could only have the passion of a man who says, "I worship God with my whole heart—I give Him everything!" David never held back. David didn't say, "Well, you know, I'm doing too much work in the church. I think I ought to let up." David went out for God 100 percent. He extended himself, and he gave himself.

My, how David loved God, and how this man served God! Will you listen to him again, because we have some glorious statements from him. If you listen carefully, maybe you can hear his heartbeat. In Psalm 108:1 he said,

> *O God, my heart is steadfast; I will sing and give praise, even with my glory.*

Oh, to have a heart that's steadfast! In effect he was saying, "I've set my sails, I'm headed in one direction and nothing will deter me. My heart is fixed—I don't care what people are saying; I don't care how people feel about me." Did you know that David even lost the affection of his wife because of his irrepressible joy and service to God? But it made no difference to this man. He was out for God 100 percent. Listen to him again:

> *Bless the LORD, O my soul; and all that is within me, bless His holy name! Bless the LORD, O my soul, and forget not all His benefits.* (Psalm 103:1–2)

If you want to know how important this event really was to David, may I say to you that at least eleven of the psalms that David wrote were written around this event of bringing up the ark to Jerusalem. Strange as it may seem to you, there are many scholars who believe that David wrote Psalm 23 at this particular time. We know that he wrote Psalm 24 also for this occasion.

Listen to his expression of joy. This is what went on in his heart, because this man had a great desire to bring the ark up to Jerusalem:

The earth is the LORD'S, and all its fullness, the world and those who dwell therein. For He has founded it upon the seas, and established it upon the waters. Who may ascend into the hill of the LORD? Or who may stand in His holy place? He who has clean hands and a pure heart, who has not lifted up his soul to an idol, nor sworn deceitfully. He shall receive blessing from the LORD, and righteousness from the God of his salvation. (Psalm 24:1–5)

Here is a very personal psalm that he wrote at this time. I also think that David must have gone ahead of the ark into Jerusalem. This is what he sang as he went:

I will extol You, O Lord, for You have lifted me up, and have not let my foes rejoice over me. O Lord my God, I cried out to You, and You healed me. O Lord, You brought my soul up from the grave; You have kept me alive, that I should not go down to the pit. Sing praise to the Lord, you saints of His, and give thanks at the remembrance of His holy name. For His anger is but for a moment, His favor is for life; weeping may endure for a night, but joy comes in the morning. (Psalm 30:1–5)

These are the thoughts that went through David's very being as he brought the ark up yonder to Jerusalem.

Now, let me make something clear. Don't get the idea that David had some superstitious notion that God was dwelling in that box-like ark. He did not. Look at Psalm 123:1 where he says, "Unto You I lift up my eyes, O You who dwell in the heavens." David understood that God dwelt in the heavens and that the ark was only the presence of God—the Shekinah glory—in their midst.

(However, I have a notion that the Shekinah glory departed when the people of Israel let the ark go into the hands of the pagan Philistines. They had disobeyed God's instructions by taking it to the actual battlefield, divorcing it from the remainder of the tabernacle.)

But when David decided to restore the ark and bring it up to Jerusalem he went all out. He had the whole orchestra out there that day:

> *Then David and all the house of Israel played music before the LORD on all kinds of instruments of fir wood, on harps, on stringed instruments, on tambourines, on sistrums, and on cymbals.* (2 Samuel 6:5)

This was the greatest event in his life, and he was praising God for it. But these festivities were marred by a serious accident. Amidst all of the celebration something tragic took place.

You see, the ark had been placed on a cart being drawn by oxen. As they went over the threshing floor of Nachon, one of the oxen stumbled and the ark shifted, so it looked as if the ark would tip and fall off the cart. Uzzah, who was driving the cart, naturally wanted to save the ark so he put forth his hand to steady it—that's all he did. Uzzah just reached out and put his hand on the ark. Notice what happened:

> *Then the anger of the LORD was aroused against Uzzah, and God struck him there for his error; and he died there by the ark of God.* (2 Samuel 6:7)

Now, three times in that verse God let us know that He was responsible for the death of Uzzah. God doesn't want us blaming Uzzah's death on anybody else, because God's shoulders are broad enough to carry all the blame for putting Uzzah to death.

Now, may I say that in this lackadaisical age in which we live—I'll be very candid with you—it seems a rather small breach of conduct for such extreme punishment, does it not? We get the impression that God has gone a little too far here. One might even argue that God had no business putting this man to death. Uzzah just wanted to help—he reached out his hand to steady the ark, then God got angry and killed him!

Well, I want you to know that this affected David. He called off the festivities, stopped the procession, and took the ark back and left it in the home of Obed-Edom, the Gittite. Notice David's reaction:

> **And David became angry because of the
> LORD'S outbreak against Uzzah; and he
> called the name of the place Perez Uzzah
> to this day.** (2 Samuel 6:8)

The Lord had placed an extreme punishment
upon Uzzah, and David didn't like it. His feeling
was, *I don't like what God has done.* Then we are
told in verse 9:

> **David was afraid of the LORD that day;
> and he said, "How can the ark of the LORD
> come to me?"**

In other words, "How could God do this when I
was just trying to do a good thing and a right
thing? I wanted to bring the ark to Jerusalem,
and now look what God has done—He killed my
man Uzzah!" So David was angry, but he was
also filled with terror and dread of the Lord that
day.

Now, let's ask the question that is in all our
minds: What was so serious about what Uzzah
did? Why was his offense treated in such a strong
manner? Wasn't God being truculent? Wasn't He
being rather stern and severe? Did He have any

right to do this? Well, let's look at some things we may have missed, and I hope that by the time we are finished you will agree that God *was* doing right when He killed Uzzah.

God had given certain instructions in dealing with the ark, and when God gives instructions, He expects them to be followed specifically and to the letter. This business today that God is just a big sob sister is irreverent. In fact, it's blasphemous. He is not that kind of God. His rule is law; it has to be followed to the very letter. If you doubt it, just try stepping off the top of a fifteen-story building. I do not care what kind of saint you happen to be—you'll meet your death on the pavement beneath, because God has a law of gravitation that we are not to violate. When we do, we pay the consequences no matter who we are. Friends, God's instructions are to be followed implicitly.

God's first rule regarding the ark was that only Levites were to serve God in the tabernacle and to carry the ark. Uzzah was a Levite, so he met that requirement. But God gave specific rules and regulations with regard to the tabernacle and the articles of furniture. Note carefully what God's Word says in Numbers 4:15:

> *And when Aaron and his sons have fin-*
> *ished covering the sanctuary and all the*
> *furnishings of the sanctuary, when the*
> *camp is set to go, then the sons of Kohath*
> *shall come to carry them; but they shall not*
> *touch any holy thing, lest they die. These*
> *are the things in the tabernacle of meeting*
> *which the sons of Kohath are to carry.*

God said that the Kohathites, a family of the Levites, would have the charge of carrying the articles of furniture in the tabernacle. But there was one thing that God wanted to make clear to them: they did not *serve* in the tabernacle, and since they did not serve they were not to touch the ark. It was hands-off. That was God's rule, God's law.

Now, there is something else. In Numbers 7:9, where the princes brought their offerings, one of the things they brought was carts for the Levites. But none was given to the Kohathites who carried the articles of furniture. Why?

> *But to the sons of Kohath he gave*
> *none, because theirs was the service of*
> *the holy things, which they carried on*
> *their shoulders.*

The Kohathites were never to carry any article of furniture on a cart. They were to carry it on their shoulders.

Going back to David's transportation of the ark, we have here two serious infractions of the Mosaic Law. First of all, they had put the ark on a cart, which was contrary to God's specific command. The second thing is that Uzzah touched it, contrary to God's command.

"But," someone may say, "the Philistines got by with that! In 1 Samuel, chapter six, we read that when the Philistines sent back the ark they put it on a cart, and nothing happened to *them*." May I say to you that God had given no law to the Philistines about the ark, so He did not hold them responsible. But Israel had God's Word, and light always creates responsibility!

So the people of Israel were in open and flagrant and direct violation of God's specific command, and they were disobeying in the presence of light. They adopted the method of the pagan Philistines. I have a notion someone said to David, "Say, the Philistines sent it back to us in a cart; let's bring it up to Jerusalem in a cart—that's easier."

Now, David recognized his error later on, and he corrected that error by bringing up the ark the right way; that is, the way God had commanded it:

> *Now it was told King David, saying, "The LORD has blessed the house of Obed-Edom and all that belongs to him, because of the ark of God." So David went and brought up the ark of God from the house of Obed-Edom to the City of David with gladness. And so it was, when those bearing the ark of the LORD had gone six paces, that he sacrificed oxen and fatted sheep.* (2 Samuel 6:12–13)

That's all the information we have in the historical Book of 2 Samuel. But when you come to the Book of Chronicles you find God's interpretation of history. If anything in the Book of Samuel really puzzles you, it's always helpful to turn over to Chronicles and find out God's interpretation of it.

After David realized his error, he became a preacher! He wanted to tell everyone the right way to go about moving the ark:

> *Then David said, "No one may carry the ark of God but the Levites, for the LORD*

*has chosen them to carry the ark of God
and to minister before Him forever."*
(1 Chronicles 15:2)

So why didn't he practice that? Well, he didn't
know at first. Now look ahead to verse 12:

*He said to them, "You are the heads of the
fathers' houses of the Levites; sanctify
yourselves, you and your brethren, that
you may bring up the ark of the LORD God
of Israel to the place I have prepared for
it. For because you did not do it the first
time, the LORD our God broke out against
us, because we did not consult Him about
the proper order." So the priests and the
Levites sanctified themselves to bring up
the ark of the LORD God of Israel. And the
children of the Levites bore the ark of God
on their shoulders, by its poles, as Moses
had commanded according to the word of
the LORD. (vv. 12-15)*

You see, David corrected his error and brought the
ark up to Jerusalem according to God's appointed
method.

My beloved, may I say to you that there is

tremendous importance in doing things God's way. It's so easy for us to read this record and blame David, censure him, and find fault with him. But we need to remember that all of these things happened for examples, and they are recorded for our lessons today.

In light of what happened to David, we need to ask ourselves a question: Is there any field today in which we are doing right things in the wrong way? There are about a hundred applications that I could make, but I don't want to be far-fetched. I want to stick to this particular passage of Scripture and not go beyond the realm of the Holy Spirit. So I will say that I see two fields today in which we are attempting to do the right thing in a wrong way. The first is according to the way of salvation. The second has to do with the way of sanctification.

There may be multitudes of people in churches across America, but actually less than 10 percent of the population of America is ever in church on any one Sunday. That certainly is a sad commentary on a so-called Christian nation. But I still believe that our churches are filled with people who honestly and sincerely want to go to heaven. In fact, I think that most people want to go to heaven. If you went out to the street, approached the average man, and asked him if he wanted to go to heaven, I think that every right-thinking person, even an atheist, would say, "If there is a God, and if there is a heaven, I certainly want to go there. I would be a madman if I did not!" I also believe that there are multitudes of people who have joined churches, gone through the required ceremonies, performed a perfunctory ritual or a liturgy thinking that doing the right thing would get them into heaven. How many people today believe that a ceremony contributes to their salvation! Their goal is all right—they want to be saved. But they're going about it in the wrong way.

Let me tell you a little story about a mountain boy out in east Tennessee. This mountain boy got converted, so the preacher came to him and said, "Now what you ought to do is be baptized." The boy said, "Well, I don't know anything about it. But if you say I should be baptized, I'm willing to do anything. I just want to be saved, but if that's what you say to do, I'll be baptized." So the preacher took the boy down to a little mountain stream that was clear as crystal. They went out into the middle of the stream, and the preacher put him under the water and brought him up again. When the boy came up he was shouting, "Hallelujah! I saw a great big catfish down there!"

You know that boy really didn't enter into the meaning of baptism. He had his mind on fishing. The thing that excited him was something else altogether.

I'm afraid a great many people today would be more excited in seeing a fish than they would be in going through some ceremony that holds no personal meaning to them at all. This is the reason that when our Lord came to this earth, He made salvation very clear. He said,

> *I am the way, the truth, and the life. No one comes to the Father except through Me.* (John 14:6)

That forever made a dead-end street out of every ism and cult, liberal or legalistic church, and anything else that says, "Do something in order to be saved." Our Lord said, "I am the way. You either have Me, or you don't have Me. You either trust Me completely, or you don't trust Me completely. You are either resting in Me, or you don't rest in Me."

Did you know that this thing we know today as Christianity was never called "Christianity" at the beginning? It was not Roman Catholicism, it was not Baptist, it was not Methodist, Presbyterian, or Pentecostal. The Bible name for Christianity at the beginning was simply *ho hodus*, meaning *the Way*.

Let's look at some Scripture references. In Acts, when Paul was still an enemy of Christ, we read:

> *Then Saul, still breathing threats and murder against the disciples of the Lord, went to the high priest and asked letters from him to the synagogues of Damascus, so that if he found any who were of THE WAY, whether men or women, he might bring them bound to Jerusalem.* (Acts 9:1–2, emphasis mine)

He didn't say, "Christians," he didn't say, "believers," he didn't say, "saints," but rather "of *the Way*." Then there was Apollos who was a great preacher, but he didn't know the gospel:

> *So he began to speak boldly in the synagogue. When Aquila and Priscilla heard him, they took him aside and explained to him THE WAY of God more accurately.* (Acts 18:26, emphasis mine)

Not "Christianity," not "the gospel," but *the Way*, my beloved! Before Christ, all nations were allowed to "walk in their own ways" (Acts 14:16). But look what it says in chapter 17:

> **Truly, these times of ignorance God over-looked, but now commands all men every-where to repent.** (Acts 17:30)

We can still choose to go our own way, but now God has revealed to us *the* Way—the Lord Jesus Christ.

Oh, how many today are trying to carry their salvation on a cart? It's inevitable that they should stumble; and when they do, how many are placing their hands on it and saying, "I'm doing the best I can"? My friends, the best you can do is not good enough for heaven! Christ did it all, and *He is the Way*. Are you trusting Him today for your salvation?

Then what about the way of sanctification? How many of us who profess the name of Jesus Christ are living defeated lives? There are many Christians today who have been so defeated in the Christian life that they now accept such defeat as the normal thing. Others are alarmed at the defeat they are experiencing. They strug-gle, and they are embarrassed, and they are also discouraged. Throughout my ministry I have talked to countless Christians who say, "I'm defeated; I have failed. I just can't live it, can't make the goal, even though I try so hard."

Listen to me now—you *can't* live the Christian life, and God never asked you to live it. On the ark of God there is written, "Hands off!" Keep your hands off the ark. Someone is sure to argue, "But I ought to at least try." But that's the trouble, friends—we try. Paul said,

> *For sin shall not have dominion over you,*
> *for you are not under law but under grace.*
> (Romans 6:14)

"But, Paul," you ask, "how can we resist and fight and struggle?" Paul's answer is that we can't resist and fight and struggle. He says that within our flesh there's not even a *desire* to do God's will, "because the carnal mind is enmity against God; for it is not subject to the law of God, nor indeed can be. So then, those who are in the flesh cannot please God" (Romans 8:7–8). But there is something we can do:

> *I beseech you therefore, brethren, by the*
> *mercies of God, that you present* [yield]

your bodies [that is, your total personalities]
a living sacrifice, holy, acceptable to God,
which is your reasonable service. (Romans
12:1)

We can surrender, we can *yield*—that's all God is
asking us to do.

We want to try, we want to get our hands in it.
But God says, "Take your hands off! You can't do
it. Let Me do it." We want to live for God, and we
know what we're to do—we are to keep the Law.
Let me ask you something. Do you know of anyone who has succeeded at keeping the Law? Your
answer is sure to be, "No." We just can't get anywhere trying to live by the Law. But that's not
what God is asking us to do. Paul said,

Reckon yourselves to be dead indeed to
sin, but alive to God in Christ Jesus our
Lord. (Romans 6:11)

We've got to be willing to take our hands off and
let God do it, reckoning ourselves to be dead. That
makes it easier, doesn't it? If you're dead, you
can't put your hands on the ark! Just fold them in
front of you, put a lily in them if you must have

something! But don't try to stick your hands in something God has said is His responsibility.

Today, we're trying to put our hand on the ark for our salvation. And we've got our hand on the ark for sanctification. God says, "Hands off! Stand still and watch the salvation of the Lord." Do you want to be saved? Well, then, stop trying to do the "right" things and come to the Lord Jesus Christ who is the Way.

And then, do you long for sanctification but say, "I'm defeated. I've struggled, and I haven't made a go of it"? When we get to that point, we can follow David's example. David recognized his error when he tried to do the right thing in his own way. And what did he do about it? He turned to God and did it God's way.

You can turn your Christian life over to Him. You can take your hands off the ark and yield yourself to Him. That's the thing to do, beloved.

CHAPTER 4

THE MOST OUTSTANDING PROPHETIC PASSAGE

What is the greatest chapter in prophecy? I believe for the best overall picture of prophecy, the one passage that probably puts down the backbone for all of prophecy is the seventh chapter of 2 Samuel. This is the great chapter in which God promised David a Son to sit on his throne. This became the theme song of every prophet, and the fact of the matter is, it's the theme song of most of the psalms. The New Testament opens with this theme. It was the message of John the Baptist: "Repent, for the kingdom of heaven is at hand." It was the message of our Lord when He began His earthly ministry; and it is the great message of the Book of the Revelation. All of this goes back and rests upon the covenant that God made with David in 2 Samuel, chapter seven.

Let's follow this together, for it is one of the great chapters of the Word of God and a chapter we ought never to get away from:

> *Now it came to pass when the king* [David] *was dwelling in his house, and the LORD had given him rest from all his enemies all around, that the king said to Nathan the prophet, "See now, I dwell in a house of cedar, but the ark of God dwells inside tent curtains." Then Nathan said to the king, "Go, do all that is in your heart, for the LORD is with you."* (2 Samuel 7:1–3)

David had built in Jerusalem a palace, and evidently it was a thing of beauty. One night, I think it happened something like this: David was in this lovely palace, and as he was lying in bed a storm came up. He heard the rain beating upon the palace outside, but David didn't feel comfortable that night under his covers. As he listened to the rain beat down, he thought, *Here I am selfishly living in a palace, and out there is the ark of*

God in a tent. That's not right. The ark of God should be in a house.

The first thing he did the next day was call in Nathan the prophet. And he said, "Nathan, I'll tell you what I've got in mind. I'm going to gather together materials, and my friend Hiram king of Tyre will help me—he will furnish a large amount of the material. And I'm going to get together a great deal of wealth—we already have a lot of gold, but I'll need to acquire more—and I'm going to build God a house."

Then Nathan did exactly what I think I would do. He said to the king, "Go, do all that is in your heart, for the LORD is with you" (v. 3). Did you know that here is a case where a prophet was wrong? God didn't want David to build Him a house, but Nathan thought He did. I have great sympathy for Nathan, because I would have said the same thing. Wouldn't you? If you went up to an elder in your church and said, "Brother, I want to build this new building for you," I don't think he would say, "Well, I've got to go and pray about it and see whether the Lord wants you to do it." No, he would probably have his hand out the minute you said it! I wouldn't blame him for that. It seems to be the normal and natural thing to do. But, you see, the response by Nathan the prophet was wrong, and God appeared to him and corrected him. The parallel passage in Chronicles presents it a little more clearly:

> *But it happened that night that the word of God came to Nathan, saying, "Go and tell My servant David, 'Thus says the LORD: "You shall not build Me a house to dwell in. For I have not dwelt in a house since the time that I brought up Israel* [from Egypt], *even to this day, but have gone from tent to tent, and from one tabernacle to another.""*
> (1 Chronicles 17:3–5)

This is without doubt one of the most wonderful statements in this section. Here God says, "I have been in a tent, that's where the people met Me, and through the wilderness march I dwelt in a tent." God identifies Himself always with His people and comes down where they are. After all, what happened some two thousand years ago in the Incarnation? God came down and He became a man, taking upon Himself a tent of flesh. So although David wanted to build God a house, God said to David, in effect, "David, I appreciate your wanting to do this. But I've always identified Myself with the people. When they were traveling through the wilderness in tents, I dwelt in a tent. And I haven't said anything about wanting to dwell anywhere else for the people to meet Me." Listen to what He said here:

> *Wherever I have moved about with all the children of Israel, have I ever spoken a word to anyone from the tribes of Israel, whom I commanded to shepherd My people Israel, saying, "Why have you not built Me a house of cedar?"* (2 Samuel 7:7)

That's quite wonderful! God told David, "I never asked anybody to build Me a house." It wasn't a commandment of God—it wasn't even a suggestion of God. This was David's idea to build God a house.

I've always appreciated in the ministry folks who think of something to support that I haven't mentioned from the pulpit. It's a joy to see them give as they feel led to a work that is worthwhile—no one suggests it to them; it is *their* idea. I think God takes note of that kind of giving, by the way. Likewise, God gives this man David credit for his idea to build a temple.

Now listen to the gracious way the Lord

dealt with David. Some folks tell me that the God of the Old Testament is a big bully, that He's rough and harsh—but notice how He dealt with David. He did get rough with David when David sinned, but in this instance God was promising this man something quite wonderful. Listen to Him:

> *Now therefore, thus shall you say to My servant David, "Thus says the LORD of hosts: 'I took you from the sheepfold, from following the sheep, to be ruler over My people, over Israel. And I have been with you wherever you have gone, and have cut off all your enemies from before you, and have made you a great name, like the name of the great men who are on the earth.'"* (vv. 8–9)

David is ranked, even in his day, as one of the great rulers of this world. He had tremendous ability. We always are blinded by the great sin in David's life, and it's too bad that it has to be there. God could have left it out, but He didn't because He paints human nature as it is. And David certainly paid for that sin! But despite his sin, this man David was a great king and a great ruler.

So God told Nathan what He didn't want David to do. Then God said what *He* would do. And this is something to take notice of. This was what God was going to agree to do:

> *Moreover I will appoint a place for My people Israel* [God is yet to give them that land, but someday He will give it to them on His own terms—not on man's terms.]*, and will plant them, that they may dwell in a place of their own and move no more; nor shall the sons of wickedness oppress them anymore, as previously, since the time that I commanded judges to be over My people Israel, and have caused you to rest from all your enemies. Also the LORD tells you that He will make you a house.* (vv. 10–11)

Isn't that lovely? And isn't that just like the Lord? David said to Nathan, "I want to build God a house," and he was ready to do it. But God said, "Nathan, you made a mistake. I'm not going to let David build Me a house. But *I'm* going to build *David* a house." Isn't that just like our Lord? You want to do something for Him, and He does something for you instead. I believe that one of the reasons some of us are so poor today is because we do so little for the Lord. We never get in a position where He can do much for us. You see, God never lets Himself get in debt to anybody. God just won't do that. We can learn a lesson from David. He wanted to do something great for God, and God did something far greater for him.

Notice how God did it here. He said this to David,

> *He will make you a house. When your days are fulfilled and you rest with your fathers, I will set up your seed after you, who will come from your body, and I will establish his kingdom. He shall build a house for My name, and I will establish the throne of his kingdom forever.* (vv. 11b–13)

God wouldn't allow David to build the temple—he was a man with bloody hands. But there was One coming in David's line who would sit on David's throne, and, friends, whatever else the "kingdom of heaven" means it means this kingdom that God vouchsafed to this man David. Now God said He would establish his kingdom, but God went beyond that and said He would establish the throne of David's kingdom *forever.*

A great many churches and denominations today are in a sad state of trying to "build a kingdom." The denomination I was in as a boy was always talking about building a kingdom—and we didn't have even a good-sized chicken coop! But we were always "building a kingdom." Now, God never called us to build a kingdom, friends. He is going to take care of that; it is His work. He will establish that kingdom on this earth someday, but right now that kingdom is actually in abeyance. In the Gospel of Matthew the kingdom of heaven is likened to a sower that went forth to sow. That's the condition in our day, and that's the reason I think the business of the church is not to build a kingdom but to sow the Word of God. For the seed is the Word of God. Number one on the agenda of God is to sow the Word of God, and I think that should be our primary business today. Building the kingdom is God's job.

Someday He will return to this earth to establish that kingdom. And you can't have a kingdom without a king, so He is the King. Jesus Christ is sitting there at God's right hand now, and the Father has said to Him, "Sit at My right hand, till I make Your enemies Your footstool" (Psalm 110:1). The throne of David is already established and intact this very minute, but Christ is waiting to move to that throne. There's no hurry, though, because that's an eternal throne, an everlasting throne. The throne of His kingdom is forever.

Now, back in 2 Samuel chapter 7, notice this verse, it's an amazing statement:

> *I will be his Father, and he shall be My son. If he commits iniquity, I will chasten him with the rod of men and with the blows of the sons of men.* (v. 14)

"I will be his Father, and he shall be My son." To me that's one of the most wonderful verses that we have in this entire passage. Because it is speaking of the Lord Jesus Christ, here is a translation that might be helpful in our understanding it: "When guilt is laid upon Him, I will chasten Him with the rod of men." That is more accurate than, "If he commits iniquity . . . ," because Jesus was without sin. He is holy, undefiled, and separate from sinners. But when He was put on the cross, He was made sin for us. We are healed from sin by His stripes. What a picture!

> *Who Himself bore our sins in His own body on the tree, that we, having died to*

sins, might live for righteousness—by whose stripes [His stripes] *you were healed.* (1 Peter 2:24)

Because the stripes He bore were not for His sin (He was not a sinner; I am!), He was taking my place. What a glorious Son of David He is!

Now will you notice God's further promise:

But My mercy shall not depart from him, as I took it from Saul, whom I removed from before you. (2 Samuel 7:15)

God said, "I'll never take My mercy away from the line of David." I'm glad God said that because if He had not promised it, I'm sure He would have taken it away, for David's line had some sinful folk. When you follow the line of David you find that Manasseh is in that line, and he was a bad egg! In fact, there are not many good kings in the entire line. David himself sinned grievously. You'd think God would have appeared to David and said "Look, David, you have sinned and it's all off. I can't use you now." Thank God He didn't do that. And I'm thankful He will not throw you overboard or throw me overboard because of our sin. If we've come to Him and trusted in His Son, our Savior, He says, "I will never leave you nor forsake you" (Hebrews 13:5). Now, He may take us to the woodshed, and a lot of us have been taken to the woodshed, haven't we? He said that's what He would do. But His mercy will *never* depart.

One year I worked with some folks who believed there will be a partial Rapture and that only the super-duper saints will be taken up. I want you to know that there is nothing that ministers to pride quite like that! Every one of them in that group thought he was one of the super-duper saints who was going out at the Rapture. And I had a sneaking feeling they thought I wasn't going to make it. I used to say to them, "I was saved by the *mercy* of God, and I'm kept by the *mercy* of God, and when the Rapture takes place I'm going out with the rest of you because of the *mercy* of God." And when I've been there ten thousand years—well, I'm going to be there because God is merciful, friends. The mercy of God—how wonderful it is!

Do *you* know the mercy of God? Or are you trying to do business with God, trying to trade in a few of your little good works (what you call good works) for your salvation? You will find that God is not open for such business. God is prepared to extend mercy to anyone who knows he's a sinner, admits he is a sinner, and will come to God and receive what He has to offer—His salvation.

> *But My mercy shall not depart from him, as I took it from Saul, whom I removed from before you. And your house and your kingdom shall be established forever before you. Your throne shall be established forever.* (2 Samuel 7:15–16)

When I was a pastor in Nashville, Tennessee, an Orthodox rabbi lived across the street from me. He was a wonderful man, and we got well-acquainted. I said to him one day, "Do you believe that the throne of David is to be established on this earth?" He answered, "Oh, yes, I believe that. The Word of God says that." So I asked, "Is there a Jew today who could claim he is in the line of David?" The rabbi shook his head, "Unfortunately, no." Then I said, "How are you going to determine who the King is?" And he looked me right straight in the eye and said, "I don't know." I said to him, "I also believe there's going to be One to sit on the throne of David, but the difference between you and me is that I think I know who He is." David will never lack one to sit on his throne because there's One up in heaven waiting today to whom the Father says: "Sit at My right hand, till I make Your enemies Your footstool." That's where Jesus Christ is today. He is yet to come and sit on David's throne.

Let's consider David's response to God's phenomenal promises:

> ***Then King David went in and sat before the LORD*** [this man loved the Lord, and he loved to spend time with Him]***; and he said: "Who am I, O Lord GOD? And what is my house, that You have brought me this far? And yet this was a small thing in Your sight, O Lord GOD; and You have also spoken of Your servant's house for a great while to come. Is this the manner of man, O Lord GOD?"*** (vv. 18–19)

Let me give you my own translation here: "O Lord God, Thou hast spoken of Thy servant's house for a great while to come, and hast regarded me in the arrangement about the Man who is to be from above, O God Jehovah." David knew that this One who was coming in his line was the One who had been marked out before by Abraham and who was marked out as "the Lamb of God who takes away the sin of the world" as far back as when Abel brought his offering to God. David knew that this One was not only to be the King, but He was to be the Savior of the world.

David continued,

> *Now, O LORD God, the word which You have spoken concerning Your servant and concerning his house, establish it forever and do as You have said.* (v. 25)

David said, "I can't understand why You've regarded me and made me king, and now You say from my line there is coming this One. I don't understand it, but I believe You and I accept it." This was so wonderful that I imagine David went back to the Lord several times and said, "Lord, did You really mean what You said?" And God assured him, "I mean it, David." For over in Psalm 89, God said to him:

> *My covenant I will not break, nor alter the word that has gone out of My lips. Once I have sworn by My holiness; I will not lie to David: his seed shall endure forever, and his throne as the sun before Me; it shall be*

*established forever like the moon, even
like the faithful witness in the sky.* (Psalm
89:34–37)

Now, friends, God said that this covenant that He
made with David is so sure that He would take
an oath on it: "I'll not lie to David. This is the
thing that I intend to do, and it's as permanent as
is the moon." Now if the moon suddenly disap-
peared from the sky, God could break this
covenant. But that's not going to happen, friends.

If we want to know David's reaction to all of
this, we need to turn to 2 Samuel 23. By this time
David was an old man. He had already given his
last words to Solomon regarding the building of
the temple.

And may I just interject something at this
juncture? I hear all the time, it's even in books,
that the temple that was eventually built was
Solomon's temple. Friends, that wasn't Solomon's
temple. Read the record all the way through, and
you'll find out it was not Solomon's temple; it was
David's temple. David is the one who gathered the
enormous amount of material, and he drew the
blueprint. Before he died, David called Solomon in
and said to him, "This is the thing I want you to
do." It wasn't Solomon's idea at all. The only

temple Solomon had was on the side of his head! It was David's temple, friends, and God gave David credit for building it. But notice what David said toward the end of his life:

> ***Although my house is not so with God*** [I've been an awful sinner, I've failed God]***, yet He has made with me an everlasting covenant, ordered in all things and secure. For this is all my salvation.*** (2 Samuel 23:5)

In other words, "My salvation rests in the fact that God has promised to send in my line One who is to sit upon the throne—my throne—and He will be the Savior of the world." If you'd met David at that time and tried to tell him what you know today about how Jesus came some two thousand years ago, I believe that David would have said, "Well, I know nothing about that what-soever." But he believed God, so he knew there was One coming who would be his Lord, One who would not only sit upon his throne but who also would be the Savior of the world.

Do you see now why this passage in 2 Samuel 7 is such an important prophecy? I could keep you reading all night until the sun comes up in the morning by turning to the prophecies of all the prophets who dealt with this subject! This was their theme song. Every prophet mentioned that there was coming One in David's line who was to sit upon the throne of David. And the sun sets on the Old Testament with the hope that the Sun of Righteousness will arise with healing in His wings. That was the only hope that the Old Testament held out—the One coming in David's line.

But four hundred years went by when the heavens were as brass. Then, one day God broke through. He said to a virgin by the name of Mary living in Nazareth, "And behold, you will conceive in your womb and bring forth a Son, and shall call His name Jesus. He will be great, and will be called the Son of the Highest; and the Lord God will give Him the throne of His father David" (Luke 1:31–32). My friends, that may not seem important to you, but it was very important in that day and it's very important in this day.

The New Testament opens like this: "The book of the genealogy of Jesus Christ, the Son of David" (Matthew 1:1). What does that mean? It means that the covenant that God made with David and all the prophecies concerning him are headed up and find their fulfillment in Jesus Christ! That makes 2 Samuel 7 the most basic, fundamental prophecy there is in the Word of God. And if you could break that promise that God made with David, then you could break the promise made in John 3:16. But you'll never be able to break either promise, because there is One today at God's right hand. And in God's own time He will come again, and He will fulfill everything that the prophets have said concerning Him.

CHAPTER 5

DAVID BEFRIENDS THE SON OF JONATHAN

I'd like you to imagine a big blank screen, about the size of a movie screen. There's nothing on it at all—it is just a plain white canvas. Now imagine there's a black dot—about twelve inches in diameter—somewhere on that screen. It doesn't matter where it is—just imagine a black dot on this white screen. As you concentrate on that little black spot and the screen, allow me to ask you a question: Which is more impressive—that vast area of white or the black spot? Which is it that draws your attention? It's the black spot, isn't it? Next, let's imagine a picture on the screen. How about a picture of a flock of sheep? Imagine a big field with hundreds of white sheep grazing. Among those white sheep I want you to imagine there is only one black sheep. When you look at that picture, which sheep do you notice? Which sheep is it that stands out above all the others? I'll guarantee you it's the black sheep that stands out.

Likewise, friends, in observing the life of David we concentrate on one big sin in his life and give sparse attention to his noble acts and his exploits of courage. We forget that most of David's life was a life in which he had a real desire to serve God. You see, that one sin of his looms up and causes all else to sink into insignificance. We see the black spot, but we do not see that wide area in his life in which this man served God. I wonder if we do not look at each other in very much the same way. We see easily each other's faults, but we do not see each other's good points very often, do we? Someone has put it like this: "There's so much good in the worst of us, and so much bad in the best of us, that it behooves some of us not to talk about the rest of us." We ought to be very careful about talking about others.

That which stands out, of course, is usually a fault and a failing; but there are many bright spots in the long life of David. From the time we met him as a young shepherd boy who slew a giant until he was an old man, wise and experienced, he was a man who could look back upon his life and write out of that experience, "The LORD is my shepherd; I shall not want." And out of the many outstanding events in his life, I do not believe you could pick one that's more lovely than the one at which we are about to look. There is a word I'd like to use to describe it: it is the word "precious." This is a *precious* event in the life of David, and it holds many spiritual lessons for us today.

Saul had been the pitiless foe and the bitter enemy of David, and after Saul died, David began to marshal his forces. According to oriental custom, which was the law of that day, the king of a new dynasty could put to death all contenders to the throne from the former dynasty. Any claimant to the throne could be removed by execution. That was the law of the day. Now according to that law, David would have been justified in putting to death any of the offspring of Saul. David, by the way, was not amiss or squeamish about putting to death those whom he wanted removed (just ask Uriah the Hittite!). So I do not believe David would have hesitated to remove any of the line of Saul, had he seen fit to do it.

Now Jonathan, who was the son of Saul and a dear friend of David, died with his father in the same battle. But Jonathan had a son who, at the death of Saul and Jonathan, had been hidden away. The reason is obvious—he was hidden away lest David would take him and kill him. The name of this boy was Mephibosheth, and he was a cripple. He was lame in his feet, so David could easily have killed him. After all, at this particular time David was beginning to consolidate the kingdom, and in order to consolidate the kingdom he had to unify it, and in order to unify it he needed to put down all areas of rebellion and remove all threats to his throne. As long as Mephibosheth lived he was a constant danger to this man David. Therefore, David had the right and the ability to remove Mephibosheth. Actually, if David had removed him, he could have more firmly established his throne and never had another vestige of rebellion. You can see how tense the air was at this particular time, how the atmosphere must have been charged. David had come to the throne, and according to custom the thing for him to do next was hunt out all the survivors of the house of Saul and exterminate them.

Let's look at what happened:

> *And there was a servant of the house of*
> *Saul whose name was Ziba. So when they*
> *had called him to David, the king said to*
> *him, "Are you Ziba?" He said, "At your ser-*
> *vice!" Then the king said, "Is there not*
> *still someone of the house of Saul, to*
> *whom I may show the kindness of God?"*
> *And Ziba said to the king, "There is still a*
> *son of Jonathan who is lame in his feet."*
> (2 Samuel 9:2–3)

May I say to you, I actually believe that Ziba betrayed Mephibosheth by revealing his hiding place, for no one knew at this particular juncture just what David would do. David may have been lying. After all, he spent probably ten years out in the dens and caves of the earth learning to live by his wits. David could have been saying this in order that he might lay hands on any survivor of the family of Jonathan. So I'm very candid in saying that I believe Ziba betrayed Mephibosheth into David's hands.

So David sent for Mephibosheth to be brought into his presence. I'm confident that some in David's court had dark and dubious thoughts as this boy was brought in—there were some, I'm sure, who believed that David would kill him. Even Mephibosheth himself, when he came before David, fully expected to be executed.

Now as I've already said, this is one of the loveliest episodes in the life of David. His life was filled with bright spots and dark spots—in fact he had a checkered career. But this is a lovely thing. I want you to notice what happened:

> *Now when Mephibosheth the son of Jonathan, the son of Saul, had come to David, he fell on his face and prostrated himself. Then David said, "Mephibosheth?" And he answered, "Here is your servant!" So David said to him, "Do not fear, for I will surely show you kindness for Jonathan your father's sake, and will restore to you all the land of Saul your grandfather; and you shall eat bread at my table continually."* (vv. 6–7)

I'll bet this boy couldn't believe his ears when David said that he was going to be kind to him. So he bowed down and said to David,

> *What is your servant, that you should look upon such a dead dog as I?* (v. 8)

My friend, when an Israelite calls himself a dog, he has called himself the lowest thing he possibly can. It's bad enough to be a dog, but Mephibosheth felt he was a dead one. He felt that his life was not worth that of a dead dog. He said, "Why in the world are you doing this for me? I'm a dead dog!"

But David put him at ease. He said to him, "Mephibosheth, you don't need to be afraid. First of all, I'm going to show you kindness—not because of who you are, but I'm going to show you kindness because of your father, Jonathan. I loved him. He was my friend, and it's for his sake I'm showing you kindness. The second thing I'm going to do is restore to you all the possessions of Saul." You see, it would naturally stand that since Saul had been removed from the throne, he'd lose all of his former possessions and his line would be removed. But David said, "Not only am I going to restore it to you, but I'm going to have Ziba and his sons and servants bring you every year the profit that comes from the increase of that land so that you will not have to take care of it."

There is a third thing David did for Mephibosheth: he gave him a place at the king's table. When telling Ziba that he was to work the land for Mephibosheth, David said:

> *You therefore, and your sons and your ser-*
> *vants, shall work the land for him, and*
> *you shall bring in the harvest, that your*
> *master's son may have food to eat. But*
> *Mephibosheth your master's son shall eat*
> *bread at my table always.* (v. 10)

You know, that's a very peculiar place for a dead dog. You ordinarily do not see dead dogs sitting at the table of a king. But David said, "This boy is going to sit at my table the rest of his life." Tremendous, is it not? It was all unexpected and, actually, it was all undeserved. And notice that the place David gave him was a place of honor; it was the table where the princes ate. And David took the crippled boy and just pushed him right up to the table and said, "From now on you can help yourself. This is your place, it's your honor. It will be your position from now on to sit here."

This is one of the loveliest things that David ever did. There are some impressive lessons here for us and some spiritual truths we ought not to miss.

First of all, a child of God recognizes that he too is crippled in his feet. I believe that every child of God knows a great deal about lame feet. We are told in Romans 3:15–16: "Their feet are swift to shed blood; destruction and misery are in their ways." That is the report from God's clinic on the human race. Our feet lead us astray. All the way through the Bible it's the feet that seem to get us into trouble. Notice what Isaiah said:

> *All we like sheep have gone astray; we have turned, every one, to his own way; and the LORD has laid on Him the iniquity of us all.* (Isaiah 53:6)

"We have turned, every one, to his own way." What a picture of the human family today. The Word of God, from Genesis to Revelation, reveals that man attempts to make his own way and insists on staggering and stumbling down that way.

> *There is a way that seems right to a man, but its end is the way of death.* (Proverbs 14:12)

Have you ever noted how closely connected in Scripture are the soul and the feet? They are together in sin, and they are put together in salvation. One of the psalmists wrote: "But as for me, my feet had almost stumbled; my steps had nearly slipped" (Psalm 73:2). David knew something about this, too. I've often wondered if he had Mephibosheth in mind when he wrote about the feet that get us in trouble—the stumbling feet, the feet that slip. After all, he saw Mephibosheth every day at his table. Every day he watched this lame boy as he hobbled in and out. And David could say, "I've got feet just like those. Before God my spiritual feet never go in the right way. My feet never lead me to God, they lead to death." In Psalm 56:13 he said,

For You have delivered my soul from death. Have You not kept my feet from falling, that I may walk before God in the light of the living?

David realized that God would save his soul and deliver his feet. Why? Because Mephibosheth was not the only one with foot trouble. David had crippled feet also. He mentioned feet again in Psalm 116:8:

For You have delivered my soul from death, my eyes from tears, and my feet from falling.

It's interesting that David acknowledged that when God saves a man, He saves his feet also. Why? Because you and I have lame feet.

Modern philosophy and humanism present another picture of man. I once heard a liberal say that Christ came to reveal the splendors of the human soul! God said, "The heart is deceitful above all things, and desperately wicked; who can know it?" (Jeremiah 17:9). Out of the heart proceed evil thoughts and a mess of bad things. May I say to you, my beloved, the Word of God does not expect to get anything good from human nature. The Word of God says through Paul, "For I know that in me (that is, in my flesh) nothing good dwells" (Romans 7:18). Paul could say that he had no confidence in the flesh. May I ask you, have you found that to be true in your life—that you today are actually spiritually crippled? That you are lame on your spiritual feet? That you are not walking well-pleasing to God?

To all who are in that desperate condition the invitation goes out: "This is the way, walk in it" (Isaiah 30:21). And what way is that? Well, in the Old Testament it was the Law. And, my beloved, the Law was never given to save any man. The Law was given to reveal to man that he is a sinner—it was a ministration of condemnation. I disagree with some of my dispensational brethren who say the Law and the Sermon on the Mount are not for today and that we shouldn't mention them. We *are* to mention them! That's God's standard. And if you are honest and will read it, you will know you've got lame feet today and that you can't walk on them. So God moves in and says, "This is the way, walk in it." Are you walking in it? Take the Ten Commandments and put them down on your life—are you walking in them today? Are you walking in the Sermon on the Mount today? You'll say, "Of course I'm not," if you are honest. You know today you are lame. And David knew about lame feet. He saw that crippled boy every day, and it reminded him of the fact that he himself had lame feet. Therefore, the Lord Jesus says,

> *I am the way, the truth, and the life. No one comes to the Father except through Me.* (John 14:6)

Let me move on; there is another wonderful lesson here. You see, David extended kindness to

Mephibosheth for the sake of Jonathan whom he loved. Do you know how deeply David loved Jonathan? Well, when word of Jonathan's death reached him, David said,

> *How the mighty have fallen in the midst*
> *of the battle! Jonathan was slain in your*
> *high places. I am distressed for you, my*
> *brother Jonathan; you have been very*
> *pleasant to me; your love to me was won-*
> *derful, surpassing the love of women.*
> (2 Samuel 1:25–26)

David and Jonathan had made a love covenant, and in that covenant Jonathan said to David, "I know that you will come to the throne, and I want to be next to you when you do. I will be your faithful follower." When David looked at Mephibosheth, he didn't see a cripple; he saw Jonathan. Mephibosheth must have looked like Jonathan, and I think David probably wept when he first saw him. But David didn't know Mephibosheth—he did what he did for him because of Jonathan. Kindness extended to a helpless person for the sake of another—that's the grace of God. My friend, when God saves you and me it's through grace.

> *For by grace you have been saved through faith, and that not of yourselves; it is the gift of God.* (Ephesians 2:8)

That's a verse we all know, but do you want to see a picture of it? Here it is in action: a crippled boy, deserving to die, brought into the presence of David and spared for the sake of Jonathan.

Paul said in Ephesians 4:32, "And be kind to one another, tenderhearted, forgiving one another, even as God in Christ forgave you." Do you know the reason why God will forgive your sins? It's not because of who you are—we are all cripples, enemies of God. The only reason you can be forgiven is because when you come to Him and trust Christ as your Savior, God looks at you and sees Christ, not you. "For when we were still without strength [we have bad feet], in due time Christ died for the ungodly" (Romans 5:6). We are saved for the sake of Another—the Lord Jesus Christ. Paul went on to say, "But God demonstrates His own love toward us, in that while we were still sinners, Christ died for us" (v. 8).

There is another great lesson for us in this episode, and I really like this one. Did you happen to notice that David said nothing about the lame feet of Mephibosheth? He didn't say, "Boy, what's the matter with you?" He didn't say, "It's too bad you're crippled." He didn't mention it at all, and he made no allusion to it. Do you know what he did? "As for Mephibosheth," said the king, "he shall eat at my table as one of the king's sons. He will sit between Absalom and Solomon as if he were one of my sons."

You know, friends, when God forgives us our sins, He *really* forgives us!

> *For I will forgive their iniquity, and their sin I will remember no more.* (Jeremiah 31:34b)

When God saves you and forgives you, He forgets your sins because they have been blotted out and covered by the blood of Christ. That is the *only* way our sins can be forgiven.

Notice also that Mephibosheth said nothing about his lame feet. May I say to you, my beloved, some Christians today take a keen delight in telling about their old days. They like to give their testimony of when they lived in sin, and they like to go over the dirty business about as often as they can. It seems as if they revel in it. There used to be a man back East who, every time he had an opportunity to give a testimony, got up and told about how he was a drunkard and a whoremonger and all those things. He'd always end up saying something about his "old black heart." Some of the wags in the church got tired of listening to him, so when they'd see him on the street they'd say, "How's your old black heart today?"

Well, then, I wonder what David and Mephibosheth *did* talk about when they got together. Lame feet? No sir. Do you know what they talked about? They likely talked about the one person whom both of them loved—Jonathan. My beloved, if you're a child of God and have confessed your sin and been forgiven, the sin question is settled, and you should remain silent about it. We should be talking about Jesus, not about our sins.

Forgetting those things which are behind and reaching forward to those things which are ahead, I press toward the goal for the prize of the upward call of God in Christ Jesus. (Philippians 3:13–14)

Now if David didn't talk about Mephibosheth's lame feet, and if Mephibosheth didn't talk about his own lame feet, what about the others present at David's table? There was a big company at the palace every day for dinner. In fact, David ran the biggest boardinghouse—all kings did in those days. The king of Persia had a thousand out for one dinner—that's quite a few to cook for! But do you know something? The others at David's table didn't talk about Mephibosheth's lame feet, either.

I would imagine that one day they saw David come in with a stranger. He was taking his time because this stranger with him was lame on both his feet. All of the captains and sergeants and privates were sitting at their tables wondering where the stranger was going to sit. When David took him up to sit at his own table, everyone wondered who this boy was. But nobody talked about his lame feet! The gossips didn't say, "Have you heard how it happened? I'm just telling you what somebody told me, but Miss So-and-So called me on the phone and told me all about Mephibosheth, and I don't think David ought to bring him in here." They didn't do that. Instead they listened to the king. They heard David praising Mephibosheth, and their hearts went out in love to this boy. You see, love "bears all things, believes all things, hopes all things, endures all things. Love never fails" (1 Corinthians 13:7–8).

As far as I know, David was never able to make Mephibosheth walk. I suppose they brought in the best doctors of that day, but he was never able to walk. This is a very important lesson for us today. My friend, if you see that you cannot walk well-pleasing to God, turn to the Lord Jesus Christ! Christ said to the man with palsy, whose friends had let him down through the roof, "Son, your sins are forgiven you . . . Arise, take up your bed and walk" (Mark 2:5, 9). David never could do that, but Jesus Christ can. And He will do it for you if you are out trying to walk on lame spiritual feet. Paul said to believers,

> *I, therefore, the prisoner of the Lord, beseech you to walk worthy of the calling with which you were called.* (Ephesians 4:1)

Christ alone is the One who can say to you, "Rise and walk," and He alone can forgive sin.

Christ is sending out an invitation today into the highways and byways and out into the streets of your town. He is saying, "Come to My table of salvation, crippled as you are, and I will feed you and make you walk." Do you recognize that you have lame feet? Are you trying to stagger and stumble along through life? May I say, there's One today who can make you walk. There's One today who has invited you to come to His table. Will you come?

CHAPTER 6

THE KING SAID
HE WAS WRONG

The superscription on many of the psalms is actually a part of the inspired Word of God. The title of Psalm 51 is self-explanatory, and it's essential to the understanding of this psalm:

> *To the Chief Musician. A Psalm of David when Nathan the prophet went to him, after he had gone in to Bathsheba.*

Now the reference is, of course, to the great blot on David's life—that is, his sin with Bathsheba. It is not my intention to go into the lurid details of David's sin. Suffice it to say that David broke two of God's commandments. He broke the seventh commandment: "You shall not commit adultery," which he did with Bathsheba. And he broke God's sixth commandment: "You shall not murder," when he arranged for Uriah, the husband of Bathsheba, to be put in the front of the battle so that he might be killed. That was a dastardly and cold-blooded deed, for Uriah was one of David's mighty men and one of his most faithful followers.

Now after this disgraceful incident, David did nothing, and he said nothing. Those who knew about it followed suit—they did nothing, they said nothing. Actually, what David had done was a common practice at that time. Adultery was business as usual down in Egypt and in Babylon, Philistia, Edom, and Moab. As a great preacher of the South said years ago, "When you put together a bunch of crooked sticks, they seem to straighten each other out." Since all these important men engaged in adultery, somehow it gave an air of making it seem not as bad as it was. But it was as bad as God said it was.

On the surface it looked as if David had gotten by with it. But David happened to be God's man, and God was not going to let him get by with it. The fact of the matter is, David was in torment. He tells us later what really went on in his heart during that interval when he kept quiet about his sin:

When I kept silent, my bones grew old through my groaning all the day long. For day and night Your hand was heavy upon me; my vitality was turned into the drought of summer. (Psalm 32:3–4)

He was a tormented man. I think that if you had been in the court of David during that period when he was silent, you would have seen him age at least twenty or thirty years. During that period in his life, he went through awful anxiety.

Now it was during this interval of David's silence that God sent Nathan in to David. Nathan demanded an audience with David regarding an urgent matter and, when he entered David's chamber, Nathan told him a story:

There were two men in one city, one rich and the other poor. The rich man had exceedingly many flocks and herds. But the poor man had nothing, except one little ewe lamb which he had bought and nourished; and it grew up together with him and with his children. It ate of his own food and drank from his own cup and lay in his bosom; and it was like a daughter to him. And a traveler came to the rich man, who refused to take from his own flock and from his own herd to prepare one for the wayfaring man who had come to him; but he took the poor man's lamb and prepared it for the man who had come to him. (2 Samuel 12:1–4)

When David heard the story, this redheaded king stood up and in righteous indignation said, "As the LORD lives, the man who has done this shall surely die!" (v. 5). And then we come to one of the most dramatic moments in the Word of God—it makes Nathan probably the bravest man in Scripture, a lot braver than David who faced Goliath. Nathan, I imagine, pointed his finger at David and said to him, "You are the man!" (v. 7).

When Nathan said this, there were three courses open to David. He could, of course, deny the charge. He could say that Nathan was entirely wrong and was attempting to smear him! Or he could have merely taken his scepter and pointed it at Nathan. Without saying a word, the guards would have understood and would have led Nathan out and summarily executed him. But may I say, in spite of these options that were open to him, there was the third, which was to admit the charge. David followed the latter course. He made a confession of it and said he was wrong. And he was not just an ordinary man—he was the king! By tradition the king can do no wrong, you know. He is above reproach, and no one dares to point the finger at the king. But Nathan did, and the interesting thing is that David openly confessed his sin.

Now, I want to backtrack for a moment and say that there are four things that can happen to a Christian when he sins. And may I say this to you, if you are a child of God and you sin, at least one of these things *must* happen, for God says it will happen.

The first thing is that you will lose the joy of your salvation. That's the first thing that happens when a Christian sins. After David confessed his sin, that is what he asked God to restore to him:

> *Restore to me the joy of Your salvation, and uphold me by Your generous Spirit.*
> (Psalm 51:12)

Now David did not say he had lost his salvation. He had not. But he had lost the *joy* of his salvation. You have no notion how miserable that man was. You see, a real child of God cannot enjoy sin. When John wrote his first epistle, talking to the child of God, he gave one of his reasons for writing the epistle: "And these things we write to you that your joy may be full" (1 John 1:4). But you cannot have fullness of joy if you have unconfessed sin in your life. That's the reason Paul said to the Ephesians, "And do not grieve the Holy Spirit of God, by whom you were sealed for the day of redemption" (Ephesians 4:30). Your salvation is sealed to the day of your redemption, but you can grieve the Holy Spirit. That is, you can grieve Him, but you can never grieve Him away. However, you can grieve Him so much that in your life there is no manifestation of Him whatsoever, and as a result your life becomes static and stale and meaningless and joyless and powerless. That happens to the child of God when he sins and does nothing about the sin in his life.

So today there are two classes of believers: those who are living with a grieved Holy Spirit and those who are living with an ungrieved Holy Spirit. Many today are in sin, and they can fool their preacher, neighbors, friends—they may even be able to fool their wives or husbands—but one thing is for sure: no one is fooling God today.

If you are in sin and you have joy, then, my friend, you ought to examine your salvation because I don't think you have the real article. You cannot have fullness of joy and have unconfessed sin in your life. And if your joy is gone, believe me, friend, you know it. You have to say with David, "When I kept silent, my bones grew old every day." There's nothing that will age a Christian like living in sin. That's the reason there are so many folk who are going to psychiatrists and so many others who are falling by the wayside. It's all a result of unconfessed sin in their lives. You see, the joy is lost.

The second thing is that either we must judge ourselves or God will judge us. Listen to David here:

> *Against You, You only, have I sinned, and done this evil in Your sight—that You may be found just when You speak, and blameless when You judge.* (Psalm 51:4)

David recognized this and took his whipping. Then when his own son, Absalom, rebelled against him, drove him out of Jerusalem, and was leading a revolution against him, poor David didn't even lift his hand to those who were against him.

Instead he said to his followers, "Don't say anything or do anything to these who are against me,
because God has permitted this to happen to me.
I know that God is punishing me."

May I say to you, either we judge ourselves
or God judges us today. In 1 Corinthians 11:31
we read,

> *For if we would judge ourselves, we would
> not be judged.*

That is, when a Christian sins he has the per-
mission of God to deal with his own sin. He can
judge it.

> *But when we are judged, we are chastened
> by the Lord, that we may not be con-
> demned with the world.* (v. 32)

In other words, Paul says that if a Christian has
unconfessed sin in his life and he won't judge it
himself, then God will move in and judge that sin.
Now someone is sure to say, "Wait just a minute,
preacher! I have seen Christians who have committed a sin and God didn't seem to do anything
about it." Well, sometimes that's the way God
moves. Note what it says in 1 Timothy 5:24: "Some

men's sins are clearly evident, preceding them to judgment, but those of some men follow later." I do not know why, but sometimes when a child of God sins and refuses to deal with it, God doesn't do anything about it right away. But that sin follows the believer to judgment and he will be judged there. God has His own reason for that. I think it may be when the sin involves another Christian because God is going to wait until they both get up there and make them settle it before Him!

When I see a child of God being punished, my feeling is not "really lay on the lash," but rather, "Lord, You've punished him enough." I'm very frank to confess that I feel like God whipped David enough. And when David became an old man, I want to say to God, "Let him alone now. Don't go on whipping him." But David never said that; he never complained. And for the rest of David's life God never took the lash off his back. But you never hear David whimper or cry aloud— he knew God was punishing him for his sin.

Now there is a third thing that can happen to a child of God when he sins. There is a sin unto death:

If anyone sees his brother sinning a sin which does not lead to death, he will ask, and He will give him life for those who commit sin not leading to death. There is sin leading to death. (1 John 5:16)

Now, this is not spiritual death at all—it has no reference to that. It is physical death. What is the sin leading to death? May I say, I do not know what it is. I think one of the reasons that God does not tell us is because it's different for each individual believer. For Ananias and Sapphira, it happened to be lying to the Holy Spirit. That is not true today in most cases, because there are those today who definitely lie to the Holy Spirit and nothing happens to them. But if I knew today what the sin leading to death was in my life, you can be sure of one thing—I'd avoid that one. But there is a sin unto death that a child of God can commit, and when he does commit it God says to that one, "Come on home." Or God will put him out of operation—He'll remove him from the place of service. God does that today, my beloved. I could name at least twenty-five men whom I've definitely seen God remove. This is something that is in operation in our day. It's like the law of gravitation in that it always works. Drop a book and it will fall right down because that law always operates. Likewise, this law always operates: there is a sin unto death. Sometimes God has to say to a child of His, "Come home, My child. I can't let you keep on committing that sin."

When David committed his sin he didn't know that would happen to him. But he prayed, "Do not cast me away from Your presence. Do not remove me, oh God! Give me another chance. I've done an awful thing and You have a right to remove me, but please don't remove me. Give me another chance!" And God did so. A child of God many times needs to cry out to God, "Oh, God, this thing I've done is terrible, but don't remove me! Don't let this thing be the cause of my undoing!" And I think many times God is gracious, as He was to David, although He may discipline, for He did whip David.

Then, my beloved, we come to the fourth thing. And this is the thing that every child of God should do when he sins:

> *If we confess our sins, He is faithful and just to forgive us our sins.* (1 John 1:9)

This is exactly what David did. He went to God and said, "For I acknowledge my transgressions, and my sin is always before me" (Psalm 51:3). He also said, "Wash me and cleanse me," and God did that. But David had to learn that God could not let him get by with sin. And God didn't.

Let's turn back to 2 Samuel 12 in which Nathan was speaking:

"'Now therefore, the sword shall never depart from your house, because you have despised Me, and have taken the wife of Uriah the Hittite to be your wife.' Thus says the LORD: 'Behold, I will raise up adversity against you from your own house; and I will take your wives before your eyes and give them to your neighbor, and he shall lie with your wives in the sight of this sun. For you did it secretly, but I will do this thing before all Israel, before the sun.'" So David said to Nathan, "I have sinned against the LORD." And Nathan said to David, "The LORD also has put away your sin; you shall not die. However, because by this deed you have given great occasion to the enemies of the LORD to blaspheme, the child also who is born to you shall surely die." (vv. 10–14)

God told David, "You caused My enemies to blaspheme—I can't let you do that, David. So you'll have to be punished." After this, David went into the privacy of his own chamber and there made his confession to his Lord and God.

That is the background of Psalm 51, one of the greatest confessions that has ever been written. By studying it we learn how we should confess our sins before the Lord.

This psalm separates very nicely into three divisions. We have, first of all, the cry of conscience and conviction of sin:

Have mercy upon me, O God, according to Your lovingkindness; according to the multitude of Your tender mercies, blot out my transgressions. Wash me thoroughly from my iniquity, and cleanse me from my sin. For I acknowledge my transgressions, and my sin is always before me. (Psalm 51:1–3)

Now sin is always complicated; it never is simple. There are four different words that are used here for *sin*. God uses many more in His Word, by the way, for sin is that which is complicated, but it is goodness that is simple.

David first called his sin "transgression." *Transgression* means stepping over the boundaries that God has established. God has put up certain boundaries in this life: He has certain physical laws, He has certain moral laws, He has certain spiritual laws. And anytime man attempts to step over them, he will have to suffer the consequences. That kind of sin is always called transgression.

Then it's called "iniquity." *Iniquity* means that which is altogether wrong. You can't excuse it; you can't offer some sort of apology; you can't in any way condone it.

Then there are two words translated as "sin." In verses 2 and 3 it is the Hebrew word *chattaah*, meaning "sin offering." In verse 4 it is *chata*, translated in the Septuagint by the Greek word *hamartano*, meaning "to miss the mark." That's all—just to miss the mark. You don't come up to God's standard. It's in that sense that all of us today are sinners. None of us come up to the standard of God. All come short of the glory of God.

And then the word *evil* used by David in verse 4 means that which is actually wrong. Now I know that in this present hour we even have ministers who are trying to condone all kinds of immorality, but let it be understood that the

Bible is very clear on what's right and what's wrong. There are questionable or gray areas, I grant. But there is also clear-cut black and clear-cut white. God is very clear on certain things, and *evil* is that which is actually wrong.

David uses all of these words to speak of the fact that he was wrong. You and I cannot begin to enter into the horror of the guilt of David. To him it was repugnant! He hated the sin and he hated himself for doing it. He felt dirty all over, his conscience was outraged, and he had a guilt complex as big as the Rock of Gibraltar. There was anguish of soul in this man! There was the cry of conscience within, pointing an accusing finger and telling David he was wrong. There was no explanation he could offer at all. Listen to him again:

> *For I acknowledge my transgressions, and my sin is always before me.* (Psalm 51:3)

In no uncertain terms, the king said he was wrong.

The second division is the cry of confession of sin and the clemency and compassion of God.

> *Against You, You only, have I sinned, and done this evil in Your sight—that You may*

***be found just when You speak, and blame-
less when You judge.*** (v. 4)

David has been criticized because he made this
statement. There are those who say he should not
have said it was a sin against God; he should
have said it was a sin against Bathsheba. Wasn't
it? It sure was. It was also a sin against his
family, for he had a family at that time. David
should have added that, so the critics say. They
also say it was a sin against the society in
Jerusalem at that time, and it was a sin against
the nation of which he was king. They are right—
it was. He was breaking God's commandment.
But, my friend, in the final analysis, sin is always
against God.

The Lord told David that his sin gave "great
occasion to the enemies of the LORD to blaspheme." For three thousand years now the critic
has been pointing his finger at the Word of God
and saying, "You mean to tell me that David is a
man after God's own heart?" I heard this in
Pershing Square in Los Angeles several years
ago. A man had gathered around him a crowd—
he was a disheveled, dirty-looking fellow, with a
leer in his voice and on his face. He said to the
crowd, "They say that God is holy!" Then he gave

a suggestive laugh, made some filthy statements about David's sin, and repeated, "They say He's a *holy* God!"

God said to David, "David, you have hurt Me, and you'll have to pay for that sin. You have caused My enemies to blaspheme Me, and because of that your child will die, and the sword will never leave your house." And it never did. To his dying day, David paid for his sin. Not only that child died but Absalom, the son whom he loved most and apparently wanted to be his successor to the throne, also died. When David heard that Absalom had been killed in battle, he wrapped his mantle about his head, walked to the top of the wall, up those winding stairs, and as he went up he cried, "O my son Absalom—my son, my son Absalom—if only I had died in your place!" (2 Samuel 18:33). May I say to you, David paid for his sin.

Now notice that David makes it very clear that this sin goes back to a sin nature. He says,

Behold, I was brought forth in iniquity, and in sin my mother conceived me. (Psalm 51:5)

Paul, recognizing that, said to believers, "Brethren, if a [Christian] man is overtaken in any trespass, you who are spiritual restore such a one in a spirit of gentleness, considering yourself lest you also be tempted" (Galatians 6:1). We all come into the world with a sin nature. The Word of God confirms this. The writer of Ecclesiastes said, "For there is not a just man on earth who does good and does not sin" (7:20).

Also in the Book of Proverbs, we read: "There is a generation that is pure in its own eyes, yet is not washed from its filthiness" (30:12). There are people who think they are all right, but they are not sensitive to their sin. They are like the man in the far North who, as he got colder, wanted to rest. He felt very comfortable sitting in the snow. But those who were with him knew what was happening to him—he was freezing to death. There are many today sitting in our churches who have grown so cold spiritually and become so comfortable that they do not realize that in God's sight they are sinners. We not only need a Savior, but we also need daily *cleansing*. Paul said, "For I know that in me (that is, in my flesh) nothing good dwells" (Romans 7:18). David, you see, went right down to the root of the matter. He confessed that he had a sin nature.

David's confession continued:

Behold, You desire truth in the inward parts, and in the hidden part You will make me to know wisdom. (Psalm 51:6)

God is not interested in what you've been through on the surface. You may be baptized and be nothing in the world but a baptized sinner, still unsaved. You may be a member of a church, but, my friend, that is all exterior. You still could be lost. God says He desires truth on the inside.

David went on:

Purge me with hyssop, and I shall be clean; wash me, and I shall be whiter than snow. (Psalm 51:7)

Here is without doubt one of the greatest passages in the Word of God. There are those who say that the reason David was forgiven was because he confessed his sin. If you say that, you've told only part of the story. In fact, you haven't told even half the story. That's not the reason. Let's again turn back to the historical record:

So David said to Nathan, "I have sinned against the LORD." And Nathan said to

David, "The LORD also has put away your sin; you shall not die." (2 Samuel 12:13)

God took the first step: He sent Nathan. I think David would still be keeping quiet if Nathan had not confronted him. You see, David did not take the first step; God took the first step.

And how was God able to forgive him? Because He had revealed Himself. Now follow this closely. God revealed Himself to the nation Israel:

The LORD, the LORD God, merciful and gracious, longsuffering, and abounding in goodness and truth, keeping mercy for thousands, forgiving iniquity and transgression and sin, by no means clearing the guilty, visiting the iniquity of the fathers upon the children and the children's children to the third and the fourth generation. (Exodus 34:6–7)

Somebody says, "Doesn't it go any further than that?" It sure does. It will keep going, but that is as far down as any man will be able to see—the third and fourth generations. But I want you to notice here two things that are conflicting and contradictory. God says He forgives iniquity and He shows mercy. Then He turns right around and says He will by no means clear the guilty. There is a paradox. But listen to David again: "Purge me with hyssop, and I shall be clean; wash me, and I shall be whiter than snow."

Hyssop is a little plant that grows on rocks in damp places. An interesting aside is a statement from a scientific journal that penicillin was found growing on hyssop. However, when referred to in the Bible, hyssop had to do with something penicillin can't cure: sin. Back in the Old Testament hyssop was used for three purposes. First, when God took the children of Israel out of Egypt, He said, "There is one thing you must do at Passover. You are to take a lamb, slay it, and take its blood in a basin out to the front door. Then use bunches of hyssop to apply the blood to the doorposts and to the lintel." Second, when God was giving instructions for cleansing a leper, He told about taking a live bird brushed with hyssop dipped in the blood of a slain bird, and then letting it fly away. This portrays the death and resurrection of Christ. Third, when the children of Israel were on the wilderness march and one of them sinned, they couldn't stop and put up the tabernacle and offer a sacrifice.

So provision was made for purification of sin by killing a red heifer, burning it along with hyssop, gathering the ashes, and taking them along on the wilderness march. When a man sinned, the ashes were put in water, then hyssop was used to sprinkle them on him. What a tremendous message! There was the application of a sacrifice that brought forgiveness.

You have to go to Calvary to find the interpretation. On the cross the Son of God said, "My God, My God, why have You forsaken Me?" (Matthew 27:46). Why did He say that? I'll tell you why. Because *God cannot by any means clear the guilty*. He cannot. He never will. And when the Lord Jesus Christ, who knew no sin, was made sin for us on the cross—when He was delivered for our offenses that we might be made the righteousness of God in Him—God had to treat Him as He *must* treat sin. Remember that God spared Abraham's son, but God did not spare His own Son when He had my sin and your sin upon Him. He had to slay Him, because God *cannot* pardon the guilty. Let's be clear on that. God *hates* sin and He will punish sin. By no means will He clear the guilty.

On the cross Jesus also said, "Father, forgive them" (Luke 23:34). How can He forgive them? How can He extend mercy to thousands? How can

He forgive iniquity? How can He forgive David? And how can He forgive you and me? The Bible is clear on this: "In Him we have redemption through His blood, the forgiveness of sins, according to the riches of His grace" (Ephesians 1:7). And every time you find forgiveness in the New Testament, the blood of Christ is responsible. God never forgives sin apart from the death of Christ. *Never.* God is not forgiving sin because He is a big-hearted old man sitting on a cloud. He forgives sin because His Son paid the penalty. And now, with open arms, He can say to you, "I can extend mercy to *you* because My Son died in your place." Oh, David knew the way into the heart of God. David said, "Purge me with hyssop," meaning the application of the death of Christ.

Notice now David's cry for cleansing and communion:

Hide Your face from my sins, and blot out all my iniquities. (Psalm 51:9)

Blot out. David needed a spot remover. Once when I was planning a trip, every little book and pamphlet I read said to be sure and take along a spot remover because I was sure to get gravy on my suit! I don't know how in the world they knew me, but I appreciate the advice because I know I'll need a spot remover. We all do.

> *Create in me a clean heart, O God, and renew a steadfast spirit within me.* (Psalm 51:10)

The word for "create" here is the same word used in Genesis 1:1—"In the beginning God created the heavens and the earth"—*bara*, which means to create out of nothing. "I need a *new* heart," David said. In other words, there was nothing in David's heart that God could use. He was not asking for a renovation or a reformation. He was asking for something new. Sometimes we hear the invitation, "Give God your heart." May I ask you, what do you think God wants with that dirty, filthy heart of yours? He doesn't want it. God is not asking anyone to give Him his heart. He wants to give you a *new* one. That's what He wants to do. That's what David asked for. Oh, my friend, let God give you a new heart.

David had another request:

> *Do not cast me away from Your presence, and do not take Your Holy Spirit from me.* (Psalm 51:11)

Now, it is my understanding that a true believer would never need to ask that, because if you are indwelt by the Spirit of God, He will never leave you. Remember—you can grieve the Holy Spirit, but you could never grieve Him away. In David's case, he had so grieved the Holy Spirit that He became inoperative in David's life. Here David was asking that the Spirit of God would continue to work in his life.

Then he said,

> *Restore to me the joy of Your salvation,*
> *and uphold me by Your generous Spirit.*
> (Psalm 51:12)

Remember, the sins of David did not cause him to lose his salvation—he lost the *joy* of his salvation, and he wanted to restore communion with God. He found out, as the prodigal son found out, that it's not nearly as much fun in the far country as it is in the Father's house.

And David wanted all of this for a purpose:

> *Then I will teach transgressors Your ways,*
> *and sinners shall be converted to You.*
> *Deliver me from the guilt of bloodshed, O*
> *God, the God of my salvation, and my*

> *tongue shall sing aloud of Your righteous-*
> *ness. O Lord, open my lips, and my mouth*
> *shall show forth Your praise . . . Then You*
> *shall be pleased with the sacrifices of*
> *righteousness.* (Psalm 51:13–15, 19)

David not only wanted to praise God, he also wanted with all his heart to please Him.

The Lord Jesus went to dinner in the home of a Pharisee. A woman who had been saved came in from the street. But Simon the Pharisee knew only of her past, and he would have passed by on the other side rather than meet her on the street. But according to the custom of the day, when he had guests she had a right to come into his house and even stand and observe. She got to the place where our Lord was reclining, and she washed His feet with her tears, wiped them with the hair of her head, kissed them, and anointed them with ointment. Simon became critical and began to find fault, but our Lord really rebuked him. He said, "When I came here you didn't even furnish Me water to wash My feet. You didn't even extend to Me the common courtesies. But this woman has not ceased to wash My feet with her tears. *She's* been forgiven—you have not." Look at Luke 7:44–48 and notice especially our

Lord's final statement to the self-righteous Pharisee:

> *Therefore I say to you, her sins, which are many, are forgiven, for she loved much. But to whom little is forgiven, the same loves little.* (Luke 7:47)

We think we are all right. My friend, God cannot clear the guilty, and He says you and I are guilty before Him. The only way He could save us was to give His Son to die. To whom much is forgiven—oh, that is the one who loves much!

What is the measure of your love? Well, it is your estimate of your own sins. When was the last time you wept over your sins? When was the last time you cried out in the night because of your failure? Thank God, there is forgiveness with Him. But there needs to be confession on our part. We need to tell God we are sorry.

Chapter 7

A MAN AFTER GOD'S OWN HEART

The critic has always found fault with David. In fact, he has used David as an example to find fault with God. The critic says there must be something wrong with a God who would say that a man like David is a man after His own heart. But the critic, when he makes a statement like that, is not presenting the full picture—he's forgetting how severely God dealt with David.

You see, in David we see what might be called "the security of the believer," for although David sinned, he did not lose his salvation. God made that very clear. But that did not mean David got by with his sin. He did not. The fact of the matter is that God took David to the woodshed and really whipped him.

That answers the question of whether God will tolerate sin in the life of one of His children. God will *not*. If you are living in sin and are getting by with it, my friend, you are *not* a child of God. God doesn't whip the devil's children—He lets them alone. He will not disturb you if you are the devil's child and are living in sin. I can say that on the authority of the Word of God.

We have moved into a time of a great moral revolution. There are preachers today saying that the whole thing is turned upside down and that anything goes today. But, friends, God's man never gets by with sin. God does not sanction immorality! The Word of God is clear on that. You cannot get by with it.

Now, it is true that David sinned grievously. He lusted after Bathsheba, who was a married woman. He saw to it that her husband was killed in battle, and then he tried to keep it all a secret. Those are serious sins, and they place a black mark on the record of David's life. Now, the critic stops there and says, "Look at what a sinful man David was—what kind of a God would say that David is His man?" But let's see what happened to David as a result of his sin, for that is where we see how God feels about sin in the life of one who is His own.

First of all, there was the illness and subsequent death of the baby born to Bathsheba:

> *And the LORD struck the child that Uriah's wife bore to David, and it became ill. David therefore pleaded with God for the child, and David fasted and went in and lay all night on the ground.* (2 Samuel 12:15–16)

David went before God and pleaded for Him to spare the little fellow's life. Finally, word was brought to David that the child was dead:

> *When David saw that his servants were whispering, David perceived that the child was dead. Therefore David said to his servants, "Is the child dead?" And they said, "He is dead." So David arose from the ground, washed and anointed himself, and changed his clothes; and he went into the house of the LORD and worshiped. Then he went to his own house; and when he requested, they set food before him, and he ate.* (vv. 19–20)

David's servants were astounded. When the child was alive, David was in sackcloth and ashes. When the child died, he should have been beside himself with grief. Instead, he got up, took a shower, changed his clothes, and then went to the house of God to worship. His servants asked for an explanation, and David responded:

> *While the child was alive, I fasted and wept; for I said, "Who can tell whether the LORD will be gracious to me, that the child may live?" But now he is dead; why should I fast? Can I bring him back again? I shall go to him, but he shall not return to me.*
> (vv. 22–23)

David knew that the little baby was saved. He said, "I will go to him someday." David knew that when death came to him, he would be reunited with his son. He could rejoice because he knew that one day he would see his son again, but this does not mean that David did not grieve the loss of the little infant.

But there was more tragedy in David's life. There is an old bromide that says, "If you're going to dance, you'll have to pay the fiddler." Likewise, if you are going to indulge in sin, you will have to pay the consequences. The Lord gives it to us straight in Galatians:

> *Do not be deceived, God is not mocked; for whatever a man sows, that he will also reap. For he who sows to his flesh will of the flesh reap corruption, but he who sows to the Spirit will of the Spirit reap everlasting life.* (Galatians 6:7–8)

There is no question that David had sown to the flesh. Don't think for one minute that he could walk away from his sin, make a sweet little confession, and that was it. David did not lose his salvation as a result of his sin (and neither will we, by the way), but sin causes a festering sore that has to be lanced. Thank God He does not give up on us, but may I say, the chickens do come home to roost.

Let me explain what I mean. David had many children by several different wives. One wife bore him two exceptionally attractive children—a daughter named Tamar and a son, Absalom. In the thirteenth and fourteenth chapters of 2 Samuel, we're told the awful story of how Tamar was raped by Amnon, her half-brother. When David found out about it he was angry, but he didn't do anything about it. David was like many other men in Scripture: he was an indulgent father who raised a bunch of kids who were bad. You would think that David would have learned from the parenting mistakes made by men like Eli and Samuel, but he did not. David was not strict enough with his children. He was angry about what Amnon had done, but, after all, what kind of an example had David set for his boys? The chickens came home to roost, friends.

Now Absalom, once he'd heard of it, plotted to kill Amnon and eventually murdered him for what he had done to Tamar. In a way, Absalom seems to be justified in what he did, since David took no action when Amnon sinned. But because he'd murdered his own brother, Absalom was forced to flee. It is my belief that Absalom was David's favorite. So David mourned for him and longed for Absalom to return. Absalom did return, eventually, but his relationship with his father was never the same again, as we shall soon see.

This was the state of David's home life, friends. All of this scandal came into the family of David because of his sin. Is it possible, knowing all of this, to believe that God will allow His children to get by with sin? I think it is obvious that

He does not. As we can see, David paid dearly for his sin. But even that was not all he suffered.

Possibly the crowning heartbreak in David's life was the disloyalty and rebellion of Absalom. In a very subtle way Absalom began to steal the hearts of the children of Israel. He was an attractive young fellow—probably like David in many ways. He was the heir apparent to the throne; that is, David would have liked for Absalom to succeed him. We find in 2 Samuel 15 that Absalom had returned to Israel and was beginning to move secretly to plot David's overthrow. This was a dastardly deed, but the chickens were coming home to roost for David.

Here is how Absalom's rebellion began:

Now Absalom would rise early and stand beside the way to the gate. So it was, whenever anyone who had a lawsuit came to the king for a decision, that Absalom would call to him and say, "What city are you from?" And he would say, "Your servant is from such and such a tribe of Israel." (2 Samuel 15:2)

Absalom stationed himself at the busiest gate of the city. When men with complaints came to the gate desiring justice, he listened to them with a great show of sympathy.

> *Then Absalom would say to him, "Look, your case is good and right; but there is no deputy of the king to hear you." Moreover Absalom would say, "Oh, that I were made judge in the land, and everyone who has any suit or cause would come to me; then I would give him justice." And so it was, whenever anyone came near to bow down to him, that he would put out his hand and take him and kiss him. In this manner Absalom acted toward all Israel who came to the king for judgment. So Absalom stole the hearts of the men of Israel.* (vv. 3–6)

Absalom was a true politician, wasn't he? This is the way men and women get elected to office today. They have no qualifications other than the fact that they are good at handshaking and backslapping. There are many preachers who use this method today. They cannot preach and they cannot teach, but they sure can slap backs. Unfortunately, that is exactly what appeals to us. As far as I can tell from the Word of God, that is the way that the Antichrist will come to power. He is going to be the greatest little back-slapper that the world has ever seen. Now Absalom was a good backslapper. He stood at the gate and said, "Oh, if I were only a judge! Then you would get justice." You can understand the appeal that kind of statement would make. Absalom was saying, "If you vote me into office, I can solve all of your problems. I will be able to take care of all the foreign and domestic affairs." That is what the politicians tell us today. Unfortunately, we listen to them, believe them, and vote for them. Then when they get into office they do not produce.

Absalom was, of course, preparing for a rebellion against David, his father. Disloyalty, I believe, is one of the gravest sins among Christians. It has always cropped up among God's people. Absalom represents Judas in the New Testament; he represents that which is disloyal to the cause of Christ. How many in our day have been betrayed by someone whom they trusted? It's a heartbreak, and it's doubly so when it's your own child. That is the case with David. This rebellion within his house was a terrible thing.

Absalom's betrayal began subtly, but eventually it gained momentum. It began to snowball, and soon there was a great company standing with Absalom. Even Ahithophel, David's counselor, was a part of it. Before David actually realized what was happening, the rebellion surfaced.

Now a messenger came to David, saying, "The hearts of the men of Israel are with Absalom." So David said to all his servants who were with him at Jerusalem, "Arise, and let us flee, or we shall not escape from Absalom. Make haste to depart, lest he overtake us suddenly and bring disaster upon us, and strike the city with the edge of the sword." (vv. 13–14)

David fled from Jerusalem. The question arises, "Why did he flee?" David loved the city of Jerusalem. Why didn't he make a stand in it? I am confident that David knew God was punishing him for his sin. I know this is true on the basis of 2 Samuel 15:25 and 26, where we are told:

Then the king said to Zadok, "Carry the ark of God back into the city. If I find favor in the eyes of the LORD, He will bring me back and show me both it and His dwelling place. But if He says thus: 'I have no delight in you,' here I am, let Him do to me as seems good to Him."

David knew that what was happening to him was judgment coming from God.

As I've already mentioned, we find in 2 Samuel 13 that Amnon committed a crime against Tamar in Jerusalem. David was disgraced by that awful thing that happened. Also, David's great sin involving Uriah and Bathsheba took place in Jerusalem. David was leaving Jerusalem this time because he knew that God was punishing him, and he did not want to see the city he built and loved become the scene of battle. But it hurt him to leave the city. As David left we are told,

So David went up by the Ascent of the Mount of Olives, and wept as he went up; and he had his head covered and went barefoot. And all the people who were with him covered their heads and went up, weeping as they went up. (v. 30)

David loved Jerusalem. He did not want it to be a place of battle; yet this city would be destroyed more than any other city because of its rebellion and sin.

Also, David left Jerusalem because he was not ready to press the issue with Absalom. It was in David's heart to spare the life of his son. He did not want harm to come to Absalom. Leaving Jerusalem put David's life in grave danger, but that was nothing new to him. David knew the wilderness and knew how to hide in it. But David wasn't concerned about the danger. He was more concerned about his relationship with his son and with God than he was about his life.

Something important happened to David as he was fleeing the city of Jerusalem:

Now when King David came to Bahurim, there was a man from the family of the house of Saul, whose name was Shimei the son of Gera, coming from there. He came out, cursing continuously as he came. And he threw stones at David and at all the servants of King David. And all the people and all the mighty men were on his right hand and on his left. Also Shimei said thus when he cursed: "Come out! Come out! You bloodthirsty man, you rogue! [He was calling David a man of the devil.] *The LORD has brought upon you all the blood of the house of Saul, in whose place you have reigned; and the LORD has delivered the kingdom into the hand of Absalom your son. So now you are caught in your own evil, because you are a bloodthirsty man!"* (2 Samuel 16:5–8)

Shimei was of the family of Saul, and he took the opportunity to curse David when he was weak. But what he said to David had some truth to it. David was a man of war—he had blood on his hands—and judgment was coming upon him. There was no question about that.

Then Abishai the son of Zeruiah said to the king, "Why should this dead dog curse my lord the king? Please, let me go over and take off his head!" (v. 9)

Abishai was a loyal captain of David, and he was all for silencing Shimei permanently. But notice David's reaction:

But the king said, "What have I to do with you, you sons of Zeruiah? So let him curse, because the LORD has said to him, 'Curse David.' Who then shall say, 'Why have you done so?'" And David said to Abishai and all his servants, "See how my son who came from my own body seeks my life. How much more now may this Benjamite? Let him alone, and let him curse; for so the LORD has ordered him." (vv. 10–11)

David was saying, "I don't mind this outsider cursing me. I do not want to take revenge on him. The thing that is happening to me is the judgment of God. What disturbs me is that it is my own boy, Absalom, who is leading the rebellion against me."

Meanwhile, Absalom had gathered together a great army from all the tribes of Israel, and they began to pursue David. Now David had spent a great deal of his life running from somebody. In this instance, he and his followers fled to a city on the east side of the Jordan River, and it was, of course, indirectly because of his own sin. When it came time for David's army to go out in battle against Absalom and his troops, David wanted to go with his men. But the army refused to let David go with them:

But the people answered, "You shall not go out! For if we flee away, they will not care about us; nor if half of us die, will

***they care about us. But you are worth ten
thousand of us now. For you are now more
help to us in the city."*** (2 Samuel 18:3)

This is one of the saddest chapters in David's
life. While the chapter involving David's sin is the
most sordid, this is the saddest because it records
the death of his dearly loved son, Absalom.
Because they have urged him not to go with them
to battle, David stationed himself at the gate, and
as each of the captains went by with his division,
David looked over and said to him, "Deal gently
for my sake with the young man Absalom" (v. 5).
In other words, "Capture him, but don't hurt
him." All the army heard him give this order. I
think some smiled, but others felt a bit resentful.
Absalom would always be a troublemaker, and
they would like to eliminate him. David, however,
loved his son and did not want him to die.

This was a civil war, and it was a terrible
thing. We had a civil war in the United States,
and we know the sadness of brother fighting
brother. David was a strategist and a general,
and Absalom did not have anyone in his group
who could match David's ability or the ability of
David's three captains. Therefore, the children of
Israel lost the battle.

The battle was fought in the forests of Ephraim, and the troops of Absalom became entangled in the woods when they attempted to flee from David's army:

For the battle there was scattered over the face of the whole countryside, and the woods devoured more people that day than the sword devoured. (v. 8)

The men became bottled in; the forest became the cause of death for many of them. This was almost the case with David's son, Absalom:

Then Absalom met the servants of David. Absalom rode on a mule. The mule went under the thick boughs of a great tere-binth tree, and his head caught in the terebinth; so he was left hanging between heaven and earth. And the mule which was under him went on. Now a certain man saw it and told Joab, and said, "I just saw Absalom hanging in a terebinth tree!" (vv. 9–10)

Joab was one of David's captains, one of his mighty men, and he had no right to lay a hand on

Absalom, especially after David had given the commandment that Absalom was not to be harmed. However, Joab was weary of all the trouble Absalom had caused, and he knew that the death of this cocky young man would end the rebellion. So Joab ignored David's orders and killed Absalom as he hung there in the tree.

What happened next is one of the most touching scenes in the Word of God. David was sitting at the gate of the city, anxiously waiting for word to be brought to him regarding Absalom. A runner finally came and said to him, "You've won—the victory is yours!" David brushed it aside and asked, "But what about my son Absalom?" But the messenger was uninformed—he didn't know that Absalom was dead. And, friends, there are many messengers running about today telling the human family that God says all is well—but all is *not* well. Man is a sinner, and he needs a Savior. The first messenger didn't have the information David really needed. But a second messenger arrived, and he had the answer to David's question:

And the king said to the Cushite, "Is the young man Absalom safe?" So the Cushite answered, "May the enemies of my lord the king, and all who rise against you to do harm, be like that young man!" (v. 32)

The Cushite had the correct information. He was gently telling David that Absalom was dead. Then follows David's mourning for his son. It is the most touching expression of grief in the Bible or in any other literature:

Then the king was deeply moved, and went up to the chamber over the gate, and wept. And as he went, he said thus: "O my son Absalom—my son, my son Absalom—if only I had died in your place! O Absalom my son, my son!" (v. 33)

This tragedy broke David's heart. He had a tender love for his son, and he was extremely grieved when the boy died. Why? There are several reasons. First of all, I do not think that David was sure about the salvation of Absalom. You recall that when David's first son by Bathsheba was sick, David fasted and prayed for him. But when the child died, David arose, bathed, went to the house of God to worship, and ate a good dinner. His servants couldn't understand his action. He made it very clear to them when he said, "I am going to him someday. He will not return to me, but it will be a great day when I go to him." He knew where the little fellow was. When Absalom died, however, David's heart broke. Why? He was not sure where his son was. Frankly, I believe that David felt his son was not right with God, and that is why he was so stricken with grief. Also, even though David was a great king, he was a poor father. I am sure David realized this. He never quite succeeded in being the father he should have been, and Absalom was only one example of this failure.

David also recognized that trouble had come upon him because of the sin he had committed. God had told him that strife would never depart from his house because of it. That is exactly what happened. Here is David—a great man; the man in whose genealogy the Lord Jesus, the Messiah, came. But, my beloved, here also is a man who paid for his sin to his dying day. Don't tell me that God closes His eyes to sin. He never does. He will judge the sin that is in the hearts and lives of those who are His own.

God never would send you the darkness,
If He felt you could bear the light.

But you would not cling to His guiding hand,
  If the way were always bright.
And you would not care to walk by faith,
  Could you always walk by sight.
So He sends you the blinding darkness,
  And the furnace of seven-fold heat.
'Tis the only way, believe me,
  To keep you close to His feet.
For 'tis always so easy to wander,
  When our lives are glad and sweet.

—Author unknown

Absalom's rebellion was the crowning crisis in David's life. From that time on David was an old man. It was at this juncture in his life, however, that David wrote a beautiful psalm—Psalm 3. I believe it will probably be the prayer of the children of Israel in the time of the Great Tribulation Period:

LORD, how they have increased who trouble me! Many are they who rise up against me. Many are they who say of me, "There is no help for him in God." But You, O LORD, are a shield for me, my glory and the One who lifts up my head. I cried to the LORD with my voice, and He heard me from His

holy hill. I lay down and slept; I awoke, for the LORD sustained me. I will not be afraid of ten thousands of people who have set themselves against me all around. Arise, O LORD; save me, O my God! For You have struck all my enemies on the cheekbone; You have broken the teeth of the ungodly. Salvation belongs to the LORD. Your blessing is upon Your people.

What an amazing prayer that is! It was David's cry when he was forced to leave Jerusalem because of the rebellion of Absalom. I hope that by now you will agree with me that David was God's man. He stands on the pages of Scripture as an example of one who was a man after God's own heart.

CHAPTER 8

THE "ONLY" PSALM

When you come face-to-face with problems that arise to block your progress, have you thought of turning to read about a man who had similar problems? David walked through the storms of life, and God gave to the world, through him, the hymnbook of the Bible. We know it as the Book of Psalms.

I'd like to focus now on Psalm 62, a great hymn and a majestic psalm. It bears a superscription that is part of Scripture. It is "To the Chief Musician," and that lends importance to it. It was not just an ordinary psalm of David, for when he composed it he sent it to the head musician. The chief musician at that time was Jeduthun, one of the three leaders of the singers. He was the choirmaster of that day. The three sons of Aaron and their families contributed these three song leaders who served in turn at the tabernacle.

David, a gifted musician, was responsible for the music of the tabernacle worship. He organized the choir and the orchestra that played the great hymns he composed. But I hasten to state, the music of David was not a product of genius. He was neither a Stephen Foster nor a George Gershwin. Stephen Foster wrote of a Kentucky Home, which he never knew, and of a Suwannee River, which he had never seen. The songs were the product of genius giving voice to dreams. David, on the other hand, wrote out of profound experience. Actually, the psalms he composed encompass his own life and set it to music. They are genuine and abiding. You would not find them making the Top 40. They would not receive a Tony Award, for they are not just ditties with catchy tunes. Their musical score was written in the blood of David. Psalm 62, which we are considering, is a striking example of this.

The Great Crisis

This song is the expression of the heart of David at the time of the greatest crisis that ever came in his life. In it you see the soul of David laid bare, and you can look into its depths as at no other time.

It is true that David had a life that was a succession of mountaintop experiences. As a boy he wrestled with a bear and a lion, and that was exciting; but this psalm does not deal with that experience. Then there was a day when he was called in from the sheepfold and anointed king. We might attempt to imagine some of the emotions of the lad as the anointing oil, poured by Samuel, ran down upon his hair. What an experience—all the way from the pasture to the palace! But this psalm is not about that. Then there was the time of great challenge when David went out as a boy against Goliath with his slingshot. But he does not refer to that in this writing. We recall the scene as he sat in the torch-lit palace, and Saul, holding a javelin, hurled it at David, missing the mark only because of David's alertness to action. Exciting? Yes, but he is not writing about that here. He spent years out in the hills and dens of the earth, encountering many a crisis peculiar to rugged living, but none of these lie in the body of this psalm. Then came a day when Saul and Jonathan were killed. Both fell in the same battle. When word was brought to David, a song acknowledging God's dealing rose from his heart, but it was not this psalm; it was another, a funeral dirge. David committed the tragic sin of his life, the sin that stood out in such a glaring fashion but, again, he does not tell of it here.

My friend, Psalm 62 does not depict any of these grave seasons in his life, but it does tell of the *greatest* crisis that came to him: he was an old man when his own son, his favorite son, the son who was more like him than any of his other sons, led a rebellion against him. And David was forced to leave the comforts of the palace and flee from Jerusalem, returning once more to the dens of the earth.

The Dramatic Moment

As you watch the old king in his flight from Jerusalem you are witnessing the highest peak or crisis in which his soul is involved in the drama of faith's supreme test. Turn back to the historical record for a moment:

So David went up by the Ascent of the Mount of Olives, and wept as he went up; and he had his head covered and went barefoot. And all the people who were

**with him covered their heads and went
up, weeping as they went up.** (2 Samuel
15:30)

That was a tragic time in the life of David. It was
his dramatic moment, his time of crisis. Thomas
Paine, a great political philosopher, wrote of "the
times that tried men's souls." This time had come
to the old king.

The Line of Betrayal

Absalom, David's son, was marching into
Jerusalem. His entry was forcing a time of decision. There were some who were choosing David;
others were choosing Absalom. It was a time
when David found who were the loyal and the
disloyal in the ranks. The betrayers and followers
were well-marked.

Of note was Ahithophel (related to David by
marriage through Bathsheba), an astute states-
man, a man of sagacity, of wonderful ability, one
upon whom David had leaned. He had deserted
and gone over to Absalom. This was the first
Benedict Arnold on record, and it broke David's
heart when he found out that this trusted man
had deserted him.

Then Ziba, the servant of Mephibosheth, came and said that his master, the son of Jonathan, had betrayed him. But David could not believe Ziba, for Ziba was two-faced and he never knew which face to believe. Therefore David was not quite sure about Mephibosheth at the time.

Then, as David fled from Jerusalem, barefoot and weeping, there stood Shimei, just outside the town of Bahurim. He was of the house of Saul, and from his store of bitter hatred for the old king he heaped cursings upon David and threw stones.

A Song Out of Testing

We see Absalom entering Jerusalem in triumph, and the same crowd that shouted to the rafters for David was now shouting deliriously for Absalom. The children of these people later were the ones who shouted, "Hosanna," to the Lord Jesus Christ and in the days following shouted, "Crucify Him!" David knew the sting of the voice of the mob, and Psalm 62 is the song of David in that moment of anxiety.

Here we find a man who had committed his way to God, one who was traveling in the spiritual stratosphere; a man who was living above the storms, shocks, and stresses of this life. And as we read this psalm, which burst forth from his heart in that hour of darkness and defeat and time of testing, we are amazed at not finding one note of discouragement, no suggestion of fear, no word of distress. There is neither rancor nor bitterness welling up in the heart of the psalmist. He sings forth a song of salvation, a paean of praise, an opus of optimism. It is a song of sanguinity, a thesis of trust, and a work of wonder. How could David write such a "Hallelujah Chorus" out of an experience so dark?

Structure of This Psalm

I do not want to be tedious, but I would like to have you note the mechanics of this psalm very briefly, for it is important that you have this understanding. The little word *selah* occurs twice here. You should not verbalize *selah* in reading the Psalms, for it is actually a kind of punctuation. It is as if you have read along in a writing and come to the end of a sentence—you have gotten to the end of the thought.

While the word *selah* occurs but twice, at the end of verses 4 and 8, it breaks the psalm into three stanzas, the first line of each stanza containing the little adverb *only*. Have you noticed that? You will find this fact if you read the New American Standard version:

> *My soul waits in silence for God only; from Him is my salvation . . . My soul, wait in silence for God only, for my hope is from Him . . . Men of low degree are only vanity, and men of rank are a lie.* (Psalm 62:1, 5, 9 NASB)

The little word *only* occurs but three other times in the psalm. I think it was Spurgeon who was the first to call this "the *only* Psalm." This does not mean that there are not 149 other psalms— there are. It is "the *only* Psalm" because of the emphasis it places upon the word *only*.

The three stanzas are divided as follows:

1. The test of faith, verses 1–4

2. The time of faith, verses 5–8

3. The triumph of faith, verses 9–12

The Test of Faith

Here we see the deep conviction that moti- vated the life of David—the currents that swept over his spirit, guiding and directing him through life. Here, for the first time, we see David's soul laid bare. While you do not see the heart of the man in the historical account, you do see him in clear view in this song of his soul. His favorite son is in rebellion, actually seeking his life, and now his enemies have come to the front. They have moved to lay hold of him that they might destroy him. Some of his friends have turned traitor. David was forced to flee, for he would not offend Jerusalem, his beloved city, by doing battle within her walls. Therefore, he left and returned to the caves of the earth. He had been dealt a cruel blow.

Weaker men have crumpled under circumstances less trying than this, but from David we hear no complaint, no condemnation, no criticism. He was committed to God and cast himself upon Him. There was nothing to say; he had no defense to offer. He said that God had permitted this thing to come to him and that the outcome of it all held no concern for him. His one concern was that he remain in the hands of God. He was undisturbed, unmoved by the things taking place around him.

No doubt there were those around David who urged that he stand his ground and thereby exhibit his faith, for he was God's anointed and God should overrule this whole matter! Not David! He said that his life was in God's hands and it seemed best that he leave Jerusalem. Beloved, while small men cried for a miracle David avowed to walk in the dark, trusting God. Oh, for a faith like that—a God-given faith! To David, what others called defeat was but a test of faith. David could retreat from Jerusalem, and it is still going to sound like a victory.

Listen to David and watch his actions as the disastrous floodwaters broke upon him:

He only is my rock and my salvation, my stronghold; I shall not be shaken. (v. 6 NASB)

We note that Zadok, the high priest, decided to go with David. He was faithful and had brought the ark, a symbol to the Israelites of God's presence in their midst, and began following David. Then the old king turned and, seeing the ark, commanded Zadok to carry it back to the city:

Then the king said to Zadok, "Carry the ark of God back into the city. If I find favor in the eyes of the LORD, He will bring me back and show me both it and His dwelling place. But if He says thus: 'I have no delight in you,' here I am, let Him do to me as seems good to Him." (2 Samuel 15:25–26)

I would love to make this great truth clear so that it will live for you! Here was a man so wholly committed to God that he turned aside from any thought of merit in the ark, clinging only to God and saying to Zadok that if it was God's will for him to come back to this city, he would be allowed to come back; if not, then he was in God's hands. He refused to attempt to force God to do anything, but determined to go the way God led, regardless of the path. Oh, to live like that today!

In Psalm 62:3 David said to his enemies,

How long will you assail a man, that you may murder him, all of you, like a leaning wall, like a tottering fence? (NASB)

Many of David's former friends had turned against him or betrayed him. Ziba, the servant of Mephibosheth, did a dastardly thing by thinking he would gain favor with David if he lied and said that Mephibosheth had deserted David. And Ahithophel, David's best friend and wisest of his counselors, went over to the other side in David's darkest hour. Here in this psalm David spoke of Ahithophel prophetically as Judas Iscariot. Ahithophel was in David's inner circle and was the man whom he leaned on, and just like Judas he turned on his master.

David said that they were running over him as a mob runs over a fence, but he also said, "It is all right as long as it is God's will. If these things must come to me as a result of my sin, I am going to accept it." Hear him in verse 4:

They have counseled only to thrust him down from his high position; they delight in falsehood; they bless with their mouth, but inwardly they curse. (NASB)

Let us understand David's action under the bitter attack of Shimei. While David was on the throne Shimei bowed like the rest of them, but when he was free to express his heart of hatred we find him cursing and hurling rocks after David as he fled from Jerusalem. David had a loyal captain by the name of Abishai, a son of Zeruiah. He said to the king: "Why should this dead dog curse my lord the king? Please, let me go over and take off his head!"

My friend, if you want an example of what the Scripture means by "'Vengeance is Mine, I will repay,' says the Lord" (Romans 12:19), listen to David as he replies to his captain:

> *But the king said, "What have I to do with you, you sons of Zeruiah? So let him curse, because the LORD has said to him, 'Curse David.' Who then shall say, 'Why have you done so?'"* (2 Samuel 16:10)

In other words, David told Abishai, "God has permitted him to curse me; you let him curse me." Have you ever stopped to think, my friend, that God has given you certain enemies for a definite purpose to test you that you might become a better Christian? Do not become alarmed at the presence of enemies and difficulties that God has permitted to cumber your path. He is not being hard on you. How we need to trust God to the extent that we would not cry out at a time like that!

The Time of Faith

The second stanza brings us to "the time of faith," and this is the entire life of any man. The moment you place your faith in Jesus Christ you are saved. It is an important moment, but we should not be majoring upon our birthday. Unfortunately, there is today a neglecting of the life of faith. It is one thing to be born; it is another thing to *live*. And it is the life of faith that counts. So David is talking about "the time of faith."

When is the time of faith? Is it on a sunny day when there is not a cloud in your sky? Is it a time when everything is going exactly right, with nothing to mar your outlook? David's answer is that the best time to trust God is at the crisis moment of your life—"My soul, wait in silence for God only, for my hope is from Him" (Psalm 62:5 NASB). This is a Bible definition of prayer, by the way.

I once had a little card sent to me bearing this message: "True prayer is the Holy Spirit speaking in the believer, through the Son, to the Father." That is prayer; it is real prayer. "My hope is from Him." David said that he was not making some wild prayer, some audacious statement—that he was not demanding that God do anything; instead David avowed, "My hope is from Him." David expected God to put into his heart the thing that He wanted done; therefore, he would be praying for the thing that was best.

We wonder again if some pious people around David might not have suggested to him that he was in such a tight place that they should have a prayer meeting. To this David would have said to them that his whole life was a life of prayer, "My hope is from Him." Here is an illustration of what Paul had in mind when he said, "Pray without ceasing" (1 Thessalonians 5:17). Now by this Paul did not mean that you are to get on your knees and remain there twenty-four hours a day. But Paul did mean for you to get on your knees and pray and then live in the expectation of that prayer for twenty-four hours every day. So David did not call a prayer meeting. In fact, the amazing thing is that this psalm has no prayer in it at all. But we find that the entire psalm is in the atmosphere of prayer. David was a man so committed to God that his life and actions were that of prayer.

Now we see this old king going out of Jerusalem; we hear him weeping. But these exterior things fade away when we glimpse the depths of his heart, for he was a man who was committed to God, and he would go with God regardless of what the outcome might be. Other men would have become bitter, but not David. He was saying something here that is tremendous:

My soul, wait in silence for God only, for my hope is from Him. He only is my rock and my salvation, my stronghold; I shall not be shaken. (Psalm 62:5–6 NASB)

"He only is my rock." That is the central truth of the psalm, and that is the central truth of David's life. That is the dynamo that ran his life. That is the thing that caused him to stand head and shoulders above other men on the horizon of history. It has caused him to cast a long shadow down the corridor of time.

When we come to the New Testament we can see what the Lord Jesus meant when He made this tremendous statement:

And whoever falls on this stone will be broken; but on whomever it falls, it will grind him to powder. (Matthew 21:44)

Christ is that stone, that Rock. There is coming a day when the stone cut out without hands will fall on this earth. Today you and I can fall on this Rock, and those who fall on it will be saved. But if you wait, it will fall on you and you will be crushed.

A little Scottish woman got up in a testimony meeting and gave this as her testimony: "You know, sometimes I tremble on the rock, but the rock never trembles under me." Are you on this Rock? Whoever falls on this Rock shall be saved. This is what Paul meant when he said,

> *For no other foundation can anyone lay than that which is laid, which is Jesus Christ.* (1 Corinthians 3:11)

David said, "He only is my Rock. He is the One I am trusting. Oh, the throne is toppling, Jerusalem is in convulsions, the people have turned against me, but I am on the Rock!" David had learned that glorious lesson.

The Triumph of Faith

We find now in Psalm 62:9 that David could say:

> *Men of low degree are only vanity, and men of rank are a lie; in the balances they go up; they are together lighter than breath.* (NASB)

He had learned that one cannot trust the mob; they could not be expected to be loyal all the time for they were fickle. He had found that men of high degree, such as Ahithophel, were not to be trusted; they could not be leaned upon. This is the first thing that a new Christian must learn: *not to look to men but to look to God.* Many new Christians have become discouraged, disappointed, and disillusioned, for they set their eyes upon a man. A young Christian once told me that he had set his eyes upon a man, and it had all but made a shipwreck of his faith. David knew all of the time that he could not trust men, so his faith was fixed utterly upon God. He rested upon a Rock that could not be moved.

Then he made the point that we cannot trust in material things either:

Do not trust in oppression, and do not vainly hope in robbery; if riches increase, do not set your heart upon them. (Psalm 62:10 NASB)

Why is it that you can trust God? David said,

Once God has spoken; twice I have heard this: that power belongs to God. (v. 11 NASB)

Friend, you can trust God because He can do anything that requires power. He has all power, and He can do anything He wants to do! We catch the thinking of the psalmist that power belongs to God. It did not reside in David. He was simply a great king because God made him a great king. Now He had permitted that David be made to leave Jerusalem, and if it was not God's will that he return, then he would not go back. But David was resigning all to God, for He is the One alone who has all power.

The mad rush to gain power is the destroying element in the world at this hour. In the effort to gain power, the bomb has been created. This form of power wreaks destruction. It is man's effort at power. But David discovered that with true power there is another element that goes with it always:

> *And lovingkindness* [mercy] *is Thine, O Lord, for Thou dost recompense a man according to his work.* (v. 12 NASB)

If you have power, you ought to be able to exercise mercy. David was saying that his God, who can exercise power, is a God who can also exercise mercy. David said to Zadok that he wanted him to take the mercy seat back to Jerusalem and place it in the tabernacle, for David knew he would find mercy with God.

At the very heart of Old Testament religion was the mercy seat. At the heart of the Christian faith today is mercy. "Come, every soul by sin oppressed—there's mercy with the Lord."[1] I think that is also what Brother George Bennard meant when he wrote: "I will cling to the old rugged cross."[2] Mercy!

Here is a little story for your thinking. Stonewall Jackson received his name at the Battle of Bull Run. General Cox had already given the command to retreat, and his men had begun to withdraw when he looked across the creek to the other side of the hill. There stood General Jackson. Cox stopped short, reversed his order, and said, "Men, look! Over there stands General Jackson like a stone wall." General Stonewall Jackson was a Christian, and he had learned what David learned: when you can say, "He only is my Rock," then you can stand adamant against the battles and issues of this life. "He only is my rock and my salvation, my stronghold; I shall not be greatly shaken."

CHAPTER 9

DAVID'S GREATEST SIN

Did you know that the greatest sin David committed had nothing in the world to do with Bathsheba? Everyone thinks that the matter of Bathsheba was a terrible sin, and I'm in that number. I agree that it was an awful sin. But if you turn to the Book of Chronicles, you will find God's perspective on things. And, friends, God does not record David's sin with Bathsheba in the Book of Chronicles! When God forgave David for that sin, He not only forgave but He also forgot it! David was washed clean of that sin. But God does record another. It is the kind of sin about which folks say, "I can't see why this was such a great sin." However, it was important to

God because it was a sin on a spiritual level. It didn't affect David's salvation one whit, but it certainly affected him and the nation of Israel in their personal relationship with God. It was David's sin of numbering the people of Israel and Judah.

Here is how it all started:

> *Now Satan stood up against Israel, and moved David to number Israel.* (1 Chronicles 21:1)

Now we have found the real culprit. This was satanic—Satan was behind this whole incident.

> *So David said to Joab and to the leaders of the people, "Go, number Israel from Beersheba to Dan, and bring the number of them to me that I may know it."* (v. 2)

You recall that Moses had taken a census of the people on two occasions. In the Book of Numbers we are told that he took a census at the beginning of the wilderness march and then again at the end of the wilderness march. There was nothing wrong with that. At least, God did not find fault with that. But in this case, for David, it was sin. Why?

There are those who say that the reason David did this was because he was proud. Well, let's read on and see if there is any evidence to support that:

> *And Joab answered, "May the LORD make His people a hundred times more than they are. But, my lord the king, are they not all my lord's servants? Why then does my lord require this thing? Why should he be a cause of guilt in Israel?"* (v. 3)

Joab was the first man to oppose the computer! Everything today is being computerized—including all of us. Just about every personal bit of information about you and me is stored in a computer somewhere right now. David wanted statistics, but, as we shall see, there is sometimes sin in statistics. Joab opposed getting these statistics because he felt that pride was at the root of it.

I am of the opinion, however, that although pride did enter into David's sin, pride was not the total explanation of the sin. My reasoning comes from this verse in Jeremiah:

> *Thus says the LORD: "Let not the wise man glory in his wisdom, let not the mighty*

*man glory in his might, nor let the rich
man glory in his riches; but let him who
glories glory in this, that he understands
and knows Me, that I am the LORD, exercising lovingkindness, judgment, and
righteousness in the earth. For in these I
delight," says the LORD.* (Jeremiah 9:23–24)

Friends, God was not pleased when David took a
census because David was not delighting in the
Lord; he was delighting in his own might. So the
thing that motivated him to number the people
was the awful sin of *unbelief.* David was trusting
numbers instead of trusting God.

Despite his better judgment, Joab followed
David's order and conducted the census of the
people.

*Nevertheless the king's word prevailed
against Joab. Therefore Joab departed
and went throughout all Israel and came
to Jerusalem. Then Joab gave the sum of
the number of the people to David. All
Israel had one million one hundred thousand men who drew the sword, and Judah
had four hundred and seventy thousand
men who drew the sword. But he did not*

count Levi and Benjamin among them, for the king's word was abominable to Joab.
(1 Chronicles 21:4–6)

In all of Israel there were 1,100,000 fighting men, and in Judah there were close to 500,000. Back when Moses had taken the census, he had a measly 603,000 men. So David had a million more men than had Moses!

What a contrast this is to David, the shepherd boy. When he came into the camp and saw the great giant strutting up and down and defying Israel, this little shepherd boy didn't take a census. He didn't count how many were in the Philistine army and then try to figure out his odds of being able to take them all out. He just said, "I'll do it." How did he have the courage? Well, he trusted the Lord. My friend, you don't feel a need for God when you have one million men standing with you. But when you are faced with a giant and have in your hands only a slingshot and five stones, you know you need God.

I'm afraid that our nation is in this same position today. How often we hear the United States praised as the greatest nation on earth! I imagine the people in the Roman Empire heard that a lot, too, as did Babylon and Greece and Egypt. Those kingdoms are long gone as great world empires. Why? Because they trusted in armies. Don't misunderstand me. Every nation needs an army to defend itself in this evil world. We are not to be fools and fanatics who say we need no protection and no army. But that is not where our confidence should be! Today people think that with our bombs and sophisticated weaponry we have no need for God. My friend, we *do* need God. People are trusting the wrong things in our day. That was David's sin—he didn't believe God would provide for him; he wanted to trust in numbers instead.

This sin of unbelief was David's greatest sin. I realize this fact does not register with many today. Just as we point the finger at David for his sin with Bathsheba, so we would point the finger at a church member who staggered into a church service while he was obviously drunk. But you could walk into a Sunday morning church service in unbelief and no one would be the wiser. And even worse, if your unbelief was known, it would not be considered a serious matter. My friend, God is telling us here that He considers unbelief to be the most serious matter. Why? Because Satan is always behind unbelief. He puts unbelief into our hearts and minds so that we will not trust God. He is always urging us to put our trust in men, in armies, in money—in anything but God.

May I say that a great many folk today trust mathematics and not the Maker. They trust the computer and not the Christ. They trust in numbers and not in the name of the Lord. That is the sin of statistics.

David learned his lesson well. Listen to him:

It is better to trust in the LORD than to put confidence in man. It is better to trust in the LORD than to put confidence in princes. (Psalm 118:8–9)

In You, O LORD, I put my trust; let me never be put to shame. (Psalm 71:1)

We need to ask ourselves these penetrating questions: Do we really trust God? Do we really believe God? The Word of God says, "But without faith it is impossible to please Him" (Hebrews 11:6). The Lord Jesus said that the Holy Spirit would convict the world of sin. What kind of sin? "Because they do not believe in Me" (John 16:9). Paul wrote, "For whatever is not from faith is sin" (Romans 14:23). This is the sin of David, and it is real sin.

David soon began to see what a terrible thing he had done:

And God was displeased with this thing; therefore He struck Israel. So David said to God, "I have sinned greatly, because I have done this thing; but now, I pray, take away the iniquity of Your servant, for I have done very foolishly." (1 Chronicles 21:7–8)

Then the Lord put before David a choice of punishment.

Then the LORD spoke to Gad, David's seer, saying, "Go and tell David, saying, 'Thus says the LORD: "I offer you three things; choose one of them for yourself, that I may do it to you."'" So Gad came to David and said to him, "Thus says the LORD: 'Choose for yourself, either three years of famine, or three months to be defeated by your foes with the sword of your enemies overtaking you, or else for three days the sword of the LORD—the plague in the land, with the angel of the LORD destroying throughout all the territory of Israel.' Now consider what answer I should take back to Him who sent me." (vv. 9–12)

David's response was tremendous. I hope you agree with me by now that David was a great man. Oh, he was human like I am and you are. He stubbed his toe, he committed sins, he had his faults, but he never lost his salvation nor his desire for fellowship with God:

And David said to Gad, "I am in great distress. Please let me fall into the hand of the LORD, for His mercies are very great; but do not let me fall into the hand of man." (v. 13)

Here was a man who had ordered the census because he was trusting in man. But then he saw what he had done. I think David was an old man at this point, and he remembered that little shepherd boy who went out with his slingshot and five smooth stones. My, how he had trusted God, and what a testimony he had then! But David was as human as we are—we trust God for salvation, but we don't trust Him for the problems of life. David looked about at his enemies and wondered if his army was big enough. He forgot for the moment that his God was big enough for all the giants and all the nations that were threatening him. So, in a lapse of faith David took a census.

How many times have you and I taken a census? We didn't really trust God, and we put our faith in something else.

But David knew his God. He said, "Don't let me fall into the hand of man. I want to fall into the hands of God." Why? Because David had learned that God is merciful. I am afraid that many of us have not learned that.

> *He has not dealt with us according to our sins, nor punished us according to our iniquities. For as the heavens are high above the earth, so great is His mercy toward those who fear Him.* (Psalm 103:10–11)

God is merciful in salvation. He holds out today salvation to a lost world. On what basis? Christ is the mercy seat. You will recall that John put it this way: "And He Himself is the propitiation for our sins, and not for ours only but also for the whole world" (1 John 2:2). What is propitiation? It is the mercy seat. God has an abundance of mercy. If you want to be saved, all you have to do is go into court with God, plead guilty, and then ask for mercy. He has plenty of mercy. That is the way He will save you. Through Christ's death on the cross there is a pardon for you, and you must claim it.

Also there is the mercy of God in providence. I look back upon my life—oh, how good He has been! He is so merciful today, not only to me but to the whole unsaved world. Why didn't He come in judgment last night? Because He is merciful. He will come some day, but He is long-suffering, He is merciful—He keeps giving time for repentance. We can lean securely on His mercy because it will never cease. The fact of His mercy is not just a momentary, happy disposition. It is not some development in His character. He didn't read *How to Win Friends and Influence People* and then decide to be merciful. It is an inherent part of His nature. For that reason David could say, "Oh, give thanks to the LORD, for He is good! For His mercy endures forever" (Psalm 136:1). So David cast himself upon God's mercy.

However, our God is a just and holy God. So when one of His children sins, He must judge that sin. David had to be judged for his sin of counting the people, but take note of what David did in response:

So the LORD sent a plague upon Israel, and seventy thousand men of Israel fell. And God sent an angel to Jerusalem to destroy it. As he was destroying, the LORD looked and relented of the disaster, and said to the angel who was destroying, "It is enough; now restrain your hand." And the angel of the LORD stood by the threshing floor of Ornan the Jebusite. Then David lifted his eyes and saw the angel of the LORD standing between earth and heaven, having in his hand a drawn sword stretched out over Jerusalem. So David and the elders, clothed in sackcloth, fell on their faces. And David said to God, "Was it not I who commanded the people to be numbered? I am the one who has sinned and done evil indeed; but these sheep, what have they done? Let Your hand, I pray, O LORD my God, be against me and my father's house, but not against Your people that they should be plagued." (1 Chronicles 21:14–17)

David doesn't complain, he doesn't mope around and talk about how unfair God is being. No—he takes full responsibility for his sin. I would say that David has changed a great deal. The time when he committed the sin with Bathsheba he wasn't going to say a word about it. He even tried to cover it up and push the blame for the death of Uriah the Hittite to someone else. Now it is different. He has learned his lesson. His soul stands absolutely naked before God. What a marvelous prayer this is. He told the Lord, "I am responsible. I did this thing. Let the judgment fall upon me." And God heard David's entreaty:

> *Therefore, the angel of the LORD commanded Gad to say to David that David should go and erect an altar to the LORD on the threshing floor of Ornan the Jebusite.* (v. 18)

When I was in Jerusalem, I walked up and down the site of that threshing floor. It is located on Mount Moriah, the place where the Mosque of Omar stands today. It is interesting to note that it is the old temple area. So here we learn that it was not actually David who chose that spot for the temple, but it was God who chose it. And David certainly concurred with Him.

> *So David went up at the word of Gad, which he had spoken in the name of the*

LORD. Now Ornan turned and saw the angel; and his four sons who were with him hid themselves, but Ornan continued threshing wheat. So David came to Ornan, and Ornan looked and saw David. And he went out from the threshing floor, and bowed before David with his face to the ground. (vv. 19–21)

Ornan was threshing wheat at his threshing floor. I was there just at the beginning of harvest season. Every afternoon the wind would come up. As I sat in our hotel room, I could look over the temple area, the site of Ornan's threshing floor. The wind really whistled through there, so much so that we had to close the doors to our room. In the days of David they would wait for that wind to come up, and then they would pitch the grain up into the air. The wind would blow away the chaff, and the good grain would fall down upon the threshing floor.

Mount Moriah is the place where Abraham offered up Isaac. And at the other end of that same ridge is Golgotha, the place of the skull, where God offered up His Son to be our Savior. When I was there, I took a picture of the pile of rock that was taken out to make the roadway up to the Damascus gate. The wall of Jerusalem goes up over that ridge. It is very high. After taking that picture, I turned right around, walked ten steps, and took a picture of Golgotha—located on the same ridge, at the same elevation. It was a continuous ridge until they put the roadway through there. You see, God chose the site of Ornan's threshing floor on Mount Moriah because that is the place where God told Abraham to offer his son, looking forward to the time of the temple sacrifices and finally to the sacrifice of the Lamb of God who takes away the sin of the world.

> *Then David said to Ornan, "Grant me the place of this threshing floor, that I may build an altar on it to the LORD. You shall grant it to me at the full price, that the plague may be withdrawn from the people." But Ornan said to David, "Take it to yourself, and let my lord the king do what is good in his eyes. Look, I also give you the oxen for burnt offerings, the threshing implements for wood, and the wheat for the grain offering; I give it all."* (vv. 22–23)

This man Ornan was very generous. He offered the property and the wheat that he was gathering, which David could use for a meal offering, and also the wood and the oxen for a burnt offering. This man offered the whole thing to David. But now listen to David:

> *Then King David said to Ornan, "No, but I will surely buy it for the full price, for I will not take what is yours for the LORD, nor offer burnt offerings with that which costs me nothing." (v. 24)*

David refused to offer to God that which cost him nothing.

> *So David gave Ornan six hundred shekels of gold by weight for the place. (v. 25)*

David paid the full price for the threshing floor.

> *And David built there an altar to the LORD, and offered burnt offerings and peace offerings, and called on the LORD; and He answered him from heaven by fire on the altar of burnt offering. (v. 26)*

David made a sacrifice to God. The fire from heaven indicated that God had accepted David's offering.

> *So the LORD commanded the angel, and he returned his sword to its sheath.* (v. 27)

The sword of judgment was sheathed. But at Golgotha, that sword pierced the side of the Lord Jesus Christ. As someone has said, "I got into the heart of God through a spear wound."

> *At that time, when David saw that the LORD had answered him on the threshing floor of Ornan the Jebusite, he sacrificed there. For the tabernacle of the LORD and the altar of the burnt offering, which Moses had made in the wilderness, were at that time at the high place in Gibeon. But David could not go before it to inquire of God, for he was afraid of the sword of the angel of the LORD.* (vv. 28–30)

I want you to see something very important here. David put this altar in the place where the temple was to be built, and he offered a sacrifice.

This is the place God met with His people. This now became the place of sacrifice. You see, David understood what a lot of church members today do not understand. David put up this altar, and he offered on it a burnt offering. That burnt offering spoke of the Person of Christ. Then he offered a peace offering, which spoke of Christ as our peace. Christ made peace by the blood of His cross. Jesus Christ is our peace. He has sprinkled His own blood on the mercy seat for us. He is our great High Priest. He has ascended into heaven and stands at the right hand of the Father. There is no access to God except through the Lord Jesus Christ. David understood this, and he offered the burnt offering and the peace offering to God.

Now remember that there was a plague going on. David had seen the angel with a drawn sword in his hand stretched out over Jerusalem. David offered sacrifices to God and called on the name of the Lord. What was he asking for? For mercy!

God is a God of mercy, of lovingkindness. But did you know that God doesn't save us by His mercy? God can't just be bighearted. He can't be a sentimental old gentleman. You see, there is a penalty that must be paid. Sin must be dealt with because God is also righteous. God can't save you by love, friend. He loves you and He will extend mercy to you, but He cannot save you that way. We are saved by *grace* through faith. What does that mean? That means that someone had to pay the penalty for our sins. God couldn't just open the back door of heaven and slip us in under cover of darkness. He cannot let down the bars of heaven. Sin must be dealt with. He cannot shut His eyes to sin in order to save us. We are guilty sinners before God, and the penalty must be paid. Jesus Christ came to pay our penalty. He is the propitiation. He is the mercy seat for you and me.

Chapter 10

THE PSALM OF AN OLD SHEPHERD

The most familiar passage in all of Scripture is unquestionably Psalm 23. The beauty of this psalm has caught the fancy of the world. No other writing has been so widely circulated, yet it is very short and very simple—only six verses, 118 words in all.

In secular literature Lincoln's "Gettysburg Address" probably corresponds best to Psalm 23 in its brevity and magnificence. That seems to be the popular thing today—to be able to write in a very brief way. Someone has said, "I do not care how much a man says if he says it in a few words." Then someone else put it like this: "If folk who do not have anything to say would refrain from saying it, it would be a better world." A prominent editor in the East has this motto on his desk: "If you have anything important to say, say it in five minutes." A lady in Florida once handed me this little bit of doggerel: "Lord, fill my mouth with worthwhile stuff and nudge me hard when I've said enough." The Lord has difficulty nudging me, I'll assure you.

This psalm is simple. It's not the language of philosophy, nor is it a treatise on theology. It's not a legal document nor a scientific instrument. It's sublimely simple and it's simply sublime.

Before we look at it there are two introductory matters that I think are essential in order to understand this psalm. First of all, it is agreed that David is the author, but did he write it when he was a shepherd boy, or did he write it when he was an old king? That, by the way, is very important to the understanding of this psalm. Dr. Frank Morgan, a personal friend and the son of G. Campbell Morgan, is the one who has given it the title, "The Psalm of the Old Shepherd," and I merely follow in his footsteps.

David the king never forgot David the shepherd boy. In fact, God would not let him forget. When God sent Nathan to give David that great covenant that He made with him in the seventh chapter of 2 Samuel, we read this in verse 8:

Now therefore, thus shall you say to My servant David, "Thus says the LORD of hosts: 'I took you from the sheepfold, from following the sheep, to be ruler over My people, over Israel.'"

When God was ready to make David not only a king but also to say that from his line was coming One to rule this entire world, He said, "I want you to remember I'm the One who took you from the sheepfold. I'm the One who took you from watching over the sheep." And that, I think, is important to see. Therefore, you do not have in Psalm 23 the musings of a green, inexperienced lad, but you have the mature deliberation of a ripe experience.

Life beat and battered and baffled and bludgeoned this man David. He lived a full life—he was a hardened soldier with blood on his hands. He was a veteran who knew victory and knew defeat. He knew privation and hardship. He had been in the sun and in the shadow. He had been tested and tried. And in this psalm you do not have the theorizing of immaturity; you have the fruit and judgment that's born of a long life. David the king, sitting on the throne, looked down the corridor of time to that shepherd boy out yonder. And he thought of himself as a sheep and of God as his Shepherd leading him from that sheepfold all the way to the throne.

Now there is a second matter of introduction that is important, and it's also vitally linked with the contents of this psalm. The psalm begins with "The Lord is my shepherd." I suppose everyone has a priority. We're hearing so much today about priorities. Well, David's priority was "The Lord is my shepherd." By what authority do you call the Lord your Shepherd? Is this a psalm for everybody, irrespective of the individual? The answer is no, it is not.

The Book of Psalms is divided very much like our songbooks are today. There is a section on salvation, songs on service, and so on. There are three shepherd psalms: Psalm 22, Psalm 23, and Psalm 24. They make a triptych, which is three pictures in one frame. When I was just a boy we always went over to my aunt's house for Christmas, and the relatives took all the beds, so they put me up in the attic. I didn't mind it because that attic had a lot of interesting things in it. One was a triptych. It was three pictures in one frame—the prodigal son coming home in the center, on the left he's going to the far country, and on the other side he's living it up in the far country. I used to study that—three pictures told one story.

We have the same situation in these three psalms. In Psalm 22 we see the Lord Jesus as the Good Shepherd. He said in John 10:11,

> *I am the good shepherd. The good shepherd gives His life for the sheep.*

In Psalm 23 we have Him as the Great Shepherd. The writer to the Hebrews said,

> *Now may the God of peace who brought up our Lord Jesus from the dead, that great Shepherd of the sheep, through the blood of the everlasting covenant, make you complete in every good work to do His will, working in you what is well pleasing in His sight, through Jesus Christ, to whom be glory forever and ever. Amen.* (Hebrews 13:20–21)

And then in Psalm 24 you have the Chief Shepherd. Peter in his first epistle said,

And when the Chief Shepherd appears, you will receive the crown of glory that does not fade away. (1 Peter 5:4)

Psalm 22 speaks of the past; Psalm 23 speaks of the present; Psalm 24 looks to the future.

Psalm 22 is the psalm of the cross; Psalm 23 is the psalm of the crook; Psalm 24 is the psalm of the crown.

You see Him dying in Psalm 22; you see Him living in Psalm 23; you see Him coming in Psalm 24.

Psalm 22 is the foundation; Psalm 23 is the manifestation; Psalm 24 is the expectation.

He is the Savior in Psalm 22; He is the Satisfier in Psalm 23; He is the Sovereign in Psalm 24.

It is my position that you must know the Savior of Psalm 22 before you can know the Shepherd of Psalm 23. I do not believe that any man can say, "The Lord is my shepherd, I shall not want," until he can say, "The Lord is my Savior."

Now let's look at Psalm 23 in detail. I believe it goes something like this: we have in the first two verses a revelation of the sanctuary of the shepherd's soul. Verses 3 and 4 are a record of the musings of the shepherd's mind. In verses 5 and 6 we have a reflection of the happiness and hope of the shepherd's heart.

A Revelation of the Sanctuary
of the Shepherd's Soul

Will you notice the first verse:

The LORD is my shepherd; I shall not want.

We have here a declaration and a deduction. "The Lord is my shepherd." I'm sure when unbelievers quote this verse they mean the Lord is *a* shepherd or *the* shepherd. But they don't mean to say personally, "The Lord is *my* shepherd." This personalization makes all the difference in the world.

A preacher friend of mine was telling about an accident he saw. He came upon the edge of it and stopped to look. Someone said, "Some boy is hurt." Well, he was interested so he looked over and saw that the "some boy" was *his* boy. He recalled, "When they said, 'It's just a boy,' I was interested but not very interested. But when I saw him, I said, 'He's *my* boy.'" *My* makes all the difference in the world. "The Lord is my shepherd, I shall not want." How can you say that?

You can say it only by the authority of His redemption—by His death and resurrection, by His grace and His mercy and His love.

I was asked many years ago to give a message at a presbytery in Cisco, Texas, on the subject of eternal security, and I took John 10 as my text. After I had finished, a rancher from San Angelo, Texas, came up to me. He said, "Young man, that was a pretty good sermon, but you don't know sheep." And I said, "Well, you tell me." So he said, "I have out on the range right now about two thousand sheep. I have a whole army of helpers out there taking care of those sheep. I have about that same number of cattle, and nobody is with them. Every cow will bring in a calf at the end of the year. We don't need to put anybody with them, but we have to put somebody with the sheep."

He continued, "A sheep is not only the most helpless creature in the world, but a sheep is the most stupid creature that God ever created. A sheep is helpless, can't defend itself. It doesn't have sharp claws, doesn't have fangs—no way of defending itself. It's not like a jackrabbit. A jackrabbit doesn't have fangs or claws either, but he can run. A sheep can't run. He can't get away from trouble. If two little sheep were to wander away from the flock, over the hill just two hundred yards, they couldn't find their way back. They're lost and you'd have to go get them. If a wolf comes along, he'll kill one of the sheep. You'd think the other little sheep would be smart and say, 'While he's eating my brother I'm going to get back to the flock,' but he doesn't do that. He just goes around saying 'baa, baa' and waits to become dessert for the wolf. A sheep is a helpless and very stupid little creature."

You know, I've thought of that many times since then. The Lord must smile when He calls us sheep because He knows all about us. Then this rancher said to me, "If a sheep is safe, it's because the sheep has a wonderful shepherd." And so when I say to you, "The Lord is my shepherd, I shall not want," I'm not bragging about Vernon McGee, because he's just a sheep. The Lord has already told me I'm stupid and helpless. He's made that clear to me. But He has made it gloriously clear that He is the Good Shepherd who today is also the Great Shepherd of the sheep. And He is able to take care of His own. How wonderful that is.

Then David said in verse 2,

He makes me to lie down in green pastures; He leads me beside the still waters.

"He makes me to lie down in green pastures."
That speaks of safety. A sheep won't lie down if
there is danger. Even the laughter of a child will
startle a sheep, and he'll get to his feet. If a sheep
is lying down, that sheep is safe. My Shepherd
makes me to lie down, and He makes me to lie
down in green pastures. No sheep will lie down in
green pastures if he's hungry. He's going to eat
the green grass until he's full, then he'll lie down.
And so you have safety and you have sufficiency
here.

"He leads me beside the still waters"—the
place where it is quiet. Sheep do not like to drink
in turbulent, muddy water. They want it to be
still and quiet. The human family needs that
too—the deep satisfaction that only the Lord
Jesus can give. I listen to some of these TV pro-
grams and I hear testimonies that say, "I trusted
Jesus and He made me successful in business, He
gave me a good job, He did this for me." My
friends, that's not what the Word of God says at
all. When people talk like that, they've missed
the entire point. He doesn't give you rest, He *is*
rest. He doesn't give you the bread of life, He *is*
the bread of life. He doesn't give you the water of
life, He *is* the water of life. Today there are those
who are running everywhere trying to find satis-

faction, but you find real satisfaction only in the Lord Jesus Christ.

The psalmist expressed that longing in Psalm 55:6, "Oh, that I had wings like a dove! I would fly away and be at rest." Oh, how many people want to fly away. So many think, *If only I could get away from this place and my problems and these people I'm with. If I could just get away and settle over yonder.* That's the reason so many folks migrated to California, isn't it? I came along with all the rest, and I'm not going back to Texas either, I'll tell you that. But no matter where you go, you will not get away from your problems.

I once heard of a woman who complained and whined about everything. Time and again she'd say, "If I could just get away from this place." Her maid got tired of hearing it and finally said, "What are you trying to get away from? Trying to get away from this lovely home, this lovely family, the lovely husband you have? No matter where you go you've got to lug yourself along. You'll be taking your skin. All of your problems and all of your difficulties will go right along with you."

Oh, to find rest in the person of Christ! The psalmist again said in Psalm 37:7, "Rest in the LORD, and wait patiently for Him." When the Lord

Jesus was announcing that the kingdom of
heaven was at hand and He was rejected as the
King, He then sent out this personal invitation,

> *Come to Me, all you who labor and are
> heavy laden, and I will* [literally, "rest you"]
> *give you rest.* (Matthew 11:28)

That's the rest of redemption.

> *Take My yoke upon you and learn from Me,
> for I am gentle and lowly in heart, and you
> will find rest for your souls.* (v. 29)

It's that soul-rest that is needed today—not just
physical, not just mental, but the rest of the soul.
Only the Great Shepherd can give that to the
human heart.

A Record of the Musings
of the Shepherd's Mind

Will you notice in verse 3,

> *He restores my soul; He leads me in the
> paths of righteousness for His name's
> sake.*

Now the soul is sheltered in the sanctuary with God, but physically and mentally we must grapple with life. We must face its problems, we must meet the issues. We can't retire into a monastery today. We are out rubbing shoulders with humanity. And so we have here the discipline and correction that the Shepherd gives. "He restores my soul; He leads me in the paths of righteousness for His name's sake." We have direction as well as discipline.

When David said, "He restores my soul," he was referring back to the awful sin that he'd committed with Bathsheba. He committed actually two terrible sins at that time. He committed adultery and he committed murder, the second one to cover up the first. And David thought he might get by with it. The fact of the matter is, when he got on his throne and the court was around him, he looked over the crowd and thought, *There's old Joab. I wonder if he knows. I don't think he does.* He looked over the whole crowd and mused, *I don't think they know.* And he sat back very comfortably.

Later on, Babylon's King Nebuchadnezzar got by with sin. But you see, David was God's man. Nebuchadnezzar could get by with it; David could not. The difference is this: God does not whip the devil's children. He whips His own. He'll take them to the woodshed, which is what He did with David.

So into the court came nosy Nathan. He came in and David spoke to him because David loved Nathan. Nathan had brought him all those wonderful messages. Nathan said, "I have a story to tell you, David." And David said, "I sure like Nathan's stories." Up to that time he did like them. So he said to him, "Go ahead, tell the story." Nathan said, "Well now, here in your kingdom there are two men. One is a very rich man. He has lambs, he has herds, he has land, he has everything. Down the road from this man is a poor man, and all he has is one little ewe lamb. One day a visitor came to see the rich man and you would think that he would send out to get one of his own little lambs. After all, he wouldn't miss it and he could use that little lamb to feed the visitor. But he doesn't do that. What he does is go and get the lamb of this poor man, and he kills it in order to feed his guest." At that, David stood to his feet and, boy, he's hot now. It's interesting how we see sin in other people, isn't it? But it's hard to see sin in ourselves. Intending to punish the offender, David stood there and asked, "Where in the kingdom is that man?" And Nathan,

I think, is the bravest man in the Bible, for he pointed his finger at David and said, "You are the man!"

Do you know what David could have done? He could have lifted that royal scepter and the soldiers would have taken Nathan out and executed him. And believe me, if he'd been in any other kingdom that's exactly what would have happened. But David bowed his head and confessed that he was indeed the guilty man. Then he went before God in that marvelous Fifty-first Psalm and prayed, "Restore to me the joy of Your salvation" (v. 12).

He didn't get by with it. God put the lash to his back and never took it off as long as David lived. And personally, I have felt like saying, "Well, Lord, You should have taken the lash off his back. You've whipped him enough." But David never said that. He never whimpered, never cried aloud at what happened. David knew that he was God's man.

A man said to me some time ago, "Oh, God is sure taking me to the woodshed." And by the way, God did take that man to the woodshed and gave him a good beating. This man said to me, "Oh, it's been terrible!" I asked, "But aren't you glad for it?" He said, "What do you mean, glad?" I said,

"Aren't you glad for it because now you know you're a child of God?"

Listen to David, "Your rod and Your staff, they comfort me" (v. 4). The rod is for discipline. When a little stubborn sheep insists on going to the side, the shepherd takes that rod and hits him over the head to get him back in line. God said to David, "Get back in line." Then there is the staff or crook. That's for direction. When David was on the throne looking back over his life he could say, "I can see that point and this point and the other point where God was leading me." Can you look back like that today? Many people can say, "God was leading me here, and God was leading me there."

Now notice something else David said here, "He leads me in the paths of righteousness." David learned that God leads only in the paths of righteousness. A young fellow who was living with a girl, not married to her, talked to me. He said, "I want to know what God's will is for my life." Since he claimed he was a Christian, I figured he should know that he and his girlfriend were violating God's Word and will, so I said, "I can tell you clearly: 'He leads me in the paths of righteousness!'" And if God is leading you, my friend, He won't lead you into sin. He never will.

The Lord tempts no one to do evil, never does. He will not lead you except in paths of righteousness. Do you want to know whether you are in God's will? If you are in sin, just put it down right now—you are *not* in the will of God because He leads in the paths of righteousness.

But there's more in the fourth verse,

Yea, though I walk through the valley of the shadow of death, I will fear no evil; for You are with me; Your rod and Your staff, they comfort me.

Now will you notice that here you have not only courage but also comfort. "Though I walk through the valley of the shadow of death, I will fear no evil; for You are with me." The entire human family today is in the shadow of death. A great many folks seem to think that "though I walk through the valley of the shadow of death" applies to some well-known figure who went through it a while back. Some people will say, "Well, those people who got on the plane that crashed a while back, they were walking in the shadow of death." They were. But you and I also are walking through the valley of the shadow of death. You see, that walk begins at the moment of your birth. You begin walking through a life in which you're in the shadow of death all the time. It's always there. You could go out tonight and be killed in an accident. You could have a heart attack. All of us are walking through the shadow of death. Someone has said, "The moment that gives us life begins to take it away from us." As we walk on, this valley gets more and more narrow. I feel now like I can touch both sides of it!

Death today is a fad. Have you ever noticed that we Americans go in for fads? Do you remember the yo-yo? All of us had yo-yos. I went to college with a yo-yo. One of my professors had a yo-yo. Everybody had a yo-yo. And then we had the hula hoop. Now I did pretty well with the yo-yo, but I did not do well with the hula hoop. My daughter did all right, but I couldn't make it there. We are faddists, today. And we Christians are faddists too. First there was the tongues movement. It went across the country and then died out. Then another fad came along—demonism. Can you remember everybody talking about demons? People were casting out demons just like you swat flies. They were around everywhere. The next kick that came along was angels. That was better than demons. We were all talking about angels. I had several women tell me or write to say that they had seen angels. They never saw angels and I haven't met anybody recently who has seen an angel but everybody was writing about them.

Do you know what the subject is now? Death! Abortion—killing all those little ones before they get here. And euthanasia—just get rid of the old people. I'm opposed to that. Yes, sir! And there's also an epidemic of suicide. There are twenty-four-hour phone lines you can call if you're thinking about suicide. It's in epidemic proportions. Why? Oh, the meaninglessness of life for multitudes today, especially among college students. They are never given a challenge so they have no reason for living, no hope at all. May I say to you that it takes courage to live today, but some folk are trying to make death a very acceptable and attractive thing.

I heard a preacher on the radio delivering a sermon on death. In fact, he made it a very pleasant affair, a nice sort of experience. May I say to you, death is horrible. There's nothing beautiful about death. "The wages of sin is death" (Romans 6:23). Death has come to us, not because God wanted it to come but because of man's sin. The doorway of death was the only way God could get man out of this sin-cursed world, but it is not a pleasant thing.

I used to ride with the undertakers to the funerals I conducted, and I carried on a "friendly warfare" with them the whole time I was there. We liked each other, and they were very nice to me. But I said, "You fellows, what a business you're in. Here you paint them up and try to make them look like they're alive. There are a lot of flowers and a lot of music. You try to cover death up, but you can't cover it up."

May I say to you, friends, death is not a pleasant thing. But for the child of God, listen to David, "Yea, though I walk through the valley of the shadow of death, I will fear no evil; for You are with me." It's terrible to die by yourself. But as someone has said, that's one thing you must do by yourself. I want to say this to you: I'm not going through the doorway of death alone. I've got Somebody who says He is going with me. He's going through that door with me so I'm not going to fear because of that. Otherwise it would be a terrible thing. And I think people ought to be told it's a terrible thing. Death is terrible unless Jesus goes with you.

Verse 4 continues,

I will fear no evil; for You are with me;
Your rod and Your staff, they comfort me.

The rod is for discipline, but the staff is for direction—and David felt them both. God disciplined him, and this says the rod comforted him. Thank God, friend, that when you get away from Him He doesn't let you be happy, does He? If you are His child, He won't let you be. That rod is there. I thank God for His rod. It hurts but He says, "Get back in line, child." That's what He says, and how wonderful this is.

A Reflection of the Happiness and Hope of the Shepherd's Heart

Notice now if you will verses 5 and 6:

You prepare a table before me in the presence of my enemies.

Some people see the Lord's Supper here, and that's all right. I do not, and I don't think David did. I think all David is saying here is that preparing a table in the presence of his enemies means victory. For what reason does God prepare the table in the presence of our enemy? For a victory feast. That's what David is talking about, by the way. And believe me, many of us need a victory feast in our lives, don't we?

Victory over passion. Victory over so many of the sins that are eating at Christians today. We need to have a table prepared in the presence of our enemy that we might have victory over these things.

Then he says,

> *You anoint my head with oil; my cup runs over.* (v. 5)

Now I don't want to become theological here because I don't think David was. But to anoint his head with oil is the anointing of the Holy Spirit. The oil was put on the priest, and that was something Israel knew a great deal about—they knew David was speaking of the anointing of the Holy Spirit.

Every believer, I think, is anointed of the Holy Spirit. This is what I mean: I believe that every believer is given a gift, and the anointing is to enable him to fulfill that gift. We need that anointing today. We do not look for a baptism. The moment you were saved you were baptized, identified with Christ in the body of believers. "For by one Spirit we were all baptized into one body" (1 Corinthians 12:13). The Holy Spirit baptizes us into the body of Christ. That's not an experience. The Lord Jesus said to His disciples, "You shall be baptized with the Holy Spirit not many days from now" (Acts 1:5). Read what happened on that day in Acts 2. Were they baptized? Yes. Does it say so? No, it doesn't say so. What does it say? "And they were all filled with the Holy Spirit" (Acts 2:4). Filling is for service, for exercising your gift. They needed to serve.

"You anoint my head with oil; my cup runs over." My, how we need running-over Christians today. Many of us are like pumps. A lot of us preachers just pump. That's the way we get up a sermon; that's the way we give a sermon; that's the way we live today. We ought to be like a fountain instead. The Lord Jesus told the woman at the well that the water He would give would be like a fountain springing up to eternal life. That's the way God wants us to be. A little girl once prayed, "Lord, I can't hold very much but I can run over a whole lot." And we need to run over a whole lot today. "You anoint my head with oil; my cup runs over." How wonderful, all of the joy of the cup running over.

Now he says in the sixth verse,

Surely goodness and mercy shall follow me all the days of my life [that's everything in

time]*; and I will dwell in the house of the
LORD forever* [that's everything in eternity].

Do you know any proposition today that beats
that? Life insurance companies don't have anything that can even touch that. Let me tell you,
this world hasn't anything today to equal that.
Everything for time: "Surely goodness and mercy
shall follow me all the days of my life." That's for
here and now. "And I will dwell in the house of
the LORD forever." That takes care of eternity.
The Lord Jesus said,

*I go to prepare a place for you. And if I go
and prepare a place for you, I will come
again and receive you to Myself; that
where I am, there you may be also.* (John
14:2–3)

My! Everything is offered to the child of God
today, and we ought to be rejoicing in that.

> *O God, our help in ages past,*
> *Our hope for years to come,*
> *Our shelter from the stormy blast,*
> *And our eternal home!*
> —Isaac Watts[1]

"The Lord is my shepherd; I shall not want." David was sitting on the throne; he's an old man now. Anybody can say, "The Lord will be my shepherd; I have not wanted." It's easy to say that. But you have to be an old shepherd looking down the corridor of time for it to have real meaning. David looked over his checkered career, a full life, and he said, "The Lord is my shepherd; I shall not want."

I thank God that after seventy-five years I can say, "The Lord is my shepherd, I shall not want." I'm not bragging about myself but, oh, I *am* bragging. I'm bragging about the Shepherd I have. He is a wonderful Shepherd!

NOTES

Chapter 2

1. "My Redeemer," words by P. P. Bliss (1838–1876). Public domain.

2. R. A. Torrey, *Why God Used D. L. Moody* (New York: Revell, 1923).

Chapter 8

1. "Only Trust Him." words by John H. Stockton (1813–1877). Public domain.

2. "The Old Rugged Cross," words by George Bennard (1873–1958). Copyright renewal in 1941. Rodeheaver Co., owner.

Chapter 10

1. "O God, Our Help," words by Isaac Watts (1674–1748). Public domain.